ENGLAND

ENGLAND

Travels Through An
Unwrecked Landscape

CANDIDA LYCETT GREEN

Photographs by Bill Burlington

PAVILION

Author's Note

The places in this book are listed in the counties to which they belong,
rather than those in which they have been bureaucratically placed. The nearest town
is mentioned, should any muddle arise.
Places open to the public are listed at the back of the book. If they are *not* listed
they are *not* open to the public. The opening times should be checked, whenever
possible, before embarking on a journey.

For to Richard Ingrams and Claire Murray Threipland

First published in Great Britain in 1996 by
PAVILION BOOKS LIMITED
26 Upper Ground, London SE1 9PD

Text copyright © Candida Lycett Green 1996
Photographs copyright © Bill Burlington 1996

Maps by Venture Graphics 1996

Designed by Bet Ayer

The moral right of the author has been asserted

The author and publishers are grateful to the following for permission to reproduce copyright
material: Faber and Faber Ltd for the extract on p.2 from 'Here' by Philip Larkin, taken from
The Whitsun Weddings; extracts on pp. 105–7 from 'Little Gidding' by T.S. Eliot, taken from
Collected Poems 1909–1962, by permission of the Eliot Estate; extract on p.168 from
'Woods' by Louis MacNeice, taken from *The Collected Poems of Louis MacNeice* edited by
E.R. Dobbs; Christopher Fry for the unpublished verse on p.101; the estate of William Plomer
and Random House UK Limited for extracts from 'Reading in the Afternoon' from *Collected
Poems* on p.1; the estate of Hilaire Belloc and Random House UK Limited for the extract
from *Complete Verse* on p. 139.

A CIP catalogue record for this book is available from the British Library.

ISBN 1 85793 681 7

Typeset in Sabon 11/15 by Textype Typesetters, Cambridge
Printed and bound in Great Britain by Biddles, Surrey

2 4 6 8 10 9 7 5 3 1

This book may be ordered by post direct from the publisher.
Please contact the Marketing Department.
But try your bookshop first.

CONTENTS

INTRODUCTION

Slow dazzling clouds recall
An irretrievable dream-England,
Visioned once in the warm light
Of half delusion, half truth:

A land of everlasting elms
Mothered by round white clouds
Dream-days, anaesthetized,
Without wheels, without wounds . . .

T HE POET William Plomer perfectly describes my search for another England. I don't suppose we English will ever stop combing hedgerows and village greens up and down the land to satisfy that ever-illusive nostalgia for a place where we can bask in contented memories of lives well spent, safe in a cocoon of unthreatened stability.

In fact, the perfection of that land of gentle apple orchards and cosy cottage firesides painted by Helen Allingham never really existed. All through the nineteenth century social and artistic commentators like Cobbett, Ruskin and William Morris were decrying the ruination of England. They harped back to an age when there were no wheels or wounds. We always think our own age is the vandalistic one, and that we are the only wreckers. Even William Plomer continues his poem:

. . . Not like that now
With jet engines overhead!
It is not easy to relax in the garden
Under a canopy of strident threats.

I am not as cynical as Plomer. This collection of essays tries to show that much of England remains unwrecked: it survives as it always has done in ordinary, unexpected and un-chocolate boxy places. The pastoral idyll is not the *only* lovable England; this is just the image which sells magazines like *Country Living* and calendars in National Trust gift shops to urban dwellers. Although a once-hymned view of St Paul's Cathedral or a stretch of meadowland at Binsey in Oxfordshire may be blocked by monoliths or under dual carriageway now, new views have been thrown up as a result. Even if our housing estates, built in the same dreary styles in every county, creep outwards from the town into the farmland, England always bursts out somehow, somewhere. Views of allotments across the railway line in Wolverhampton or of fields beyond the giant cooling towers near Pontefract are as beautiful to some as any crescent in Bath or valley in Gloucestershire. Look at Hull, which Philip Larkin loved so well.

> Swerving east, from rich industrial shadows
> And traffic all night north; swerving through fields
> Too thin and thistled to be called meadows,
> And now and then a harsh-named halt, that shields
> Workmen at dawn; swerving to solitude
> Of skies and scarecrows, haystacks, hares and pheasants,
> And the widening river's slow presence,
> The piled gold clouds, the shining gull-marked mud,
>
> Gathers to the surprise of a large town:
> Here domes and statues, spires and cranes cluster
> Beside grain-scattered streets, barge-crowded water,
> And residents from raw estates, brought down
> The dead straight miles by stealing flat-faced trolleys,
> Push through plate-glass swing doors to their desires –
> Cheap suits, red kitchen-ware, sharp shoes, iced lollies,
> Electric mixers, toasters, washers, driers –

It was Richard Ingrams' idea to start a column in the *Oldie* called 'Unwrecked England'. He was offering to pay me to indulge in my favourite pastime – exploring England. (The writing about it afterwards is hell, and always will be.) I have an insatiable appetite for discovery and an uncontrollable imagination. I think that every postman I see *might* have a letter for me, and I never give up hope that at the end of a long-forgotten track I will find a nice old lady in an ancient manor house who will say, 'I've been waiting for you to come . . . I would like to leave my house to you.' Until I was sixteen I wanted to be an archaeologist – all part of my dream of finding something hitherto undiscovered; something wonderful in a forgotten, unregarded place.

For years now I have taken five days off in spring and again in early autumn to travel across different bits of England by horse. I only go by horse because I am lazy and hate walking, and riding is second nature to me. It is also a means of carrying Ordnance Survey maps, hair-drier, topographical books, Ribena, etc. Before most of them left home, Rupert and I would take the children in a covered wagon, usually along the Ridgeway or through the Cotswolds, but in recent years I have always ventured out with the same friend – the perfect travelling companion. We talk sparingly, we like looking at exactly the same things and plan to ride through every county over the next twenty years. As surfers are on a search for the perfect wave, so we are on a never-ending search for the perfect track.

We tie our horses to the lychgate and visit every church on the way, we buy postcards in every village shop and stop at good-looking pubs and hostelries when we feel like it. We have been from Brighton to Marlborough, from Marlborough to St Germans in Cornwall (in three stints), from Clun to the Forest of Dean, round the Lincolnshire and Yorkshire Wolds and from Milton Keynes to Salisbury, and are just about to ride through Leicestershire and Nottinghamshire. I read maps at night like other people read novels. We travel few roads, mostly lanes and tracks. It is different from travelling by car because we arrive at the *back* of places and see new, unexpected views. We came to Abbotsbury in Dorset over a crest of downland and saw the sea and the village below at the end of our winding track; we reached

Helmingham in Suffolk across the ancient park. We have threaded our way through the back streets of occasional towns like Louth or Aylesbury. This is how I discovered that within a stone's throw of a gigantic conurbation like the latter, or still within earshot of the motorway's low moan, there are wonderful bits of England.

The thrill of the journey, with the long road in my eye and hope in my heart, never abates. The only Beatles song I ever really went weak at the knees over was 'The long and winding road'. There is always the possibility of something unexpected happening. Both my husband Rupert and my daughter Imogen have an inability to get to a train on time. Imogen admitted to me the other day that she actually secretly *wanted* to miss trains because then that would lead her to a different, unexpected set of circumstances – anything to avoid inevitability. Certainly travelling by horse leads you into countless unforeseen situations, but a strange train journey can be equally thrilling. When I decided to go to Appledore in Kent, on a cheap, leisurely day return from Didcot, it was, for me, just as pleasurable an excursion as travelling from Baghdad to Damascus might have been to Colin Thubron. You lose all your safe terms of reference: you can imagine changing your life and settling in Rye; you can go and have tea in a village and be somebody else altogether. I enjoyed the tea shop in Barnard Castle so much that I would willingly have stayed in that town for a month.

The geographical locations of the places I have written about favour, I am afraid, where I live (Wiltshire), my spiritual home (Cornwall), and the home of our best friends (Norfolk). I have tried, on various journeys, using various methods of transport – from canal barge, or horse-drawn covered wagon to an agonizing child's bike which would not change from first gear from West Acre to Castle Acre – to touch on most counties. I am deeply conscious of missing out Bedfordshire, which I know to be packed with hidden glories, and likewise Leicestershire, Rutland, Cheshire and Staffordshire. I am so sorry.

I have tried to give an impression of each area and reveal the glory of what is always there, just below the surface. I have an ongoing argument with a particular friend who laughs when I say I would rather spend my summer in Shropshire or Dorset than in Corfu or Provence. He *will* not believe me and thinks I am being fey. I know that I am at my happiest when I have a sense of belonging in familiar England. When I made a film about gardens ten years ago there was a lady who lived in the lodge to Brocklesbury Park in Lincolnshire. She said, 'People are *always* looking for something, and it's right there under their noses.' I remain, like Ruskin, the archetypal Anglophile, who will always be faithful to 'Blind, tormented, unwearied, marvellous England'.

THE ACRES

Norfolk

THE VALLEY of the river Nar is wide, shallow and beautiful where it winds between the Acres in this undulating stretch of Norfolk. The Peddar's Way, an ancient track which starts on the north coast and streaks straight as a die towards Bury St Edmunds, crosses the Nar close by and often, at the beginning of each year, locals have heard the sound of marching troops on the track – ghosts of the Roman centurions changing posts.

Bicycling or walking from the village of West Acre to South Acre and on to Castle Acre, by the back road beside the river on a warm evening, is an idyllic and undemanding journey. West Acre is a quiet little place with deep banks and a spreading chestnut tree on its triangular village green beside the great flint church. There is a graceful medieval two-storey gatehouse of flint with stone dressings; through the grand archway you can see a red-brick eighteenth-century farmhouse standing among the fragments of what was once a larger Augustinian priory than that at Castle Acre. One of its most treasured possessions was a relic of St Andrew – a piece of his finger set in silver. This was pawned before the Dissolution of the Monasteries for £40. The village is set out in a straggling circle – cottages, a post office and a small red-brick villa with a large plaque across its façade saying 'DISTRICT NURSES HOUSE 1954'.

Down a gentle slope, past the village pub, the lane becomes a sandy track which fords the wide and trout-filled Nar. It leads across a gorse-scattered, rabbit-holed common. The land in this area is famously poor and for centuries local farmers have gleaned little from it. A long straight stretch of road follows to South Acre, where a pretty, bow-fronted, red-brick rectory with a good garden stands among chestnut trees across the way from one of the loveliest churches in Norfolk, nestling against a backdrop of huge limes and sycamores.

It has not been altered much since the fifteenth century and inside it is triple-aisled, light and graceful, with pale washed-out woodwork, clear-glass and oil lamps on the pew ends, discreetly converted to electricity. The chancel benches are made from local oak with poppy heads and panels carved by the Reverend Edmund Daubeny at the beginning of the century. He also carved the eagle lectern, which is a copy of the brass one in Norwich Cathedral. Along the north wall lies the effigy of a Knight Templar with a lion at his feet and in the north-side chapel is a tremendous alabaster and marble monument of Sir Edward Barkham and his wife. He lies recumbent, holding a book and wearing over his armour a fur-lined robe and the chain of office of the Lord Mayor of London. On either side of a macabre panel of broken skulls and bones are the kneeling figures of his two sons and three daughters. There is also a brass memorial to Sir John Harsyke (who died in 1384) holding hands with his wife Katherine. At the west end towers an extraordinary fifteenth-century font which has been restored by the Pilgrim Trust. The gaveyard is romantically unkempt to exactly the right degree.

If you travel on along the road and down a flower-banked lane past a tall, three-storey farmhouse, you will reach a shallow ford and narrow footbridge, from which unfolds one of the lordliest views in England. A sheep-filled meadow slopes up from the river to what was the Clunic priory of Castle Acre, now the finest monastic remains in East Anglia. Their setting is sylvan and romantic. The beautiful west front of the priory church is covered with a filigree of interlaced Norman arches and is flanked by the Prior's Lodging, which still has many of its rooms intact. The gentle and pastoral atmosphere of the place is all-encompassing.

At the top of the steep lane from the ford the imposing church of St James towers like a miniature cathedral. The churchyard is mown and strimmed to look like a Wilton carpet, and the interior of the fifteenth-century church feels nothing like South Acre. It has been over-restored and has lost the rich patina of centuries. If you walk on along the wide, brick-housed square with lime trees in its midst you can sit outside the Albert pub with a drink and watch the passers-by of Castle Acre, which almost amounts to a small town.

Just beyond the roofs to the east are the remains of one of the grandest castles in England – great mounds and ramparts begun just after the Norman Conquest by the Conqueror's son-in-law. The only actual building to survive is the arched gateway with small towers on each side which heralds the main village street and leads away down to the river again.

APPLEDORE

Kent

YOU CAN get to Appledore on a branch line from Ashford, rattling and swaying above flat fields, through cuttings of oak and ash and striking out deeper and deeper into Kent. After Ham Street, spread around with anonymous-looking and chimneyless new houses, you get your first sight of Romney Marsh, the 'Sixth Continent', that strange area of a hundred square miles closely bound by the sea of which it was once part. The Grand Military Canal cuts beside the line along the north side of the marsh and is filled with yellow water-lilies and swans. It was built in 1804 in an effort to fend off Napoleon and is angled every so often so that a gun emplacement could guard each stretch. It runs for twenty-three miles from Hythe to Pett.

When I got out of the train at Appledore Station there was a warm wind through high willows beside the platform. Sheep grazed in an old orchard below huge leaning apple trees. There was a neat little brick station building, a railway hotel opposite and a mile's walk to Appledore village itself. It stands on a rise above reclaimed marshland (which villagers still refer to as 'the sea'; the low hills behind are known as 'the cliff'. The main street is wide and generous and lined with cosy and comfortable eighteenth- and ninetenth-century brick cottages and houses, snug behind hedges, railings and Irish yews. Outside Tuckers, a long, low, Georgian farmhouse, dark-red hollyhocks touch the eaves and a pink mallow bush is as high as the roof itself. Beyond the Red Vine pub is the church of St Peter and St Paul – squat, stalwart and medieval – which has survived for 700 years despite being burned by the French in 1380 and bombed by the Germans in the Second World War. Wide, double-aisled and wonderful inside, it has a good 1920s stained-glass window at the west end in memory of Joseph Pearson of Park House.

You would be hard to pushed to find a more perfect Miss Marplelike village than Appledore in the whole of England. As I emerged from the tree-enclosed churchyard on to the street I witnessed a slow-motion car crash in which two very bad lady drivers scratched each other's bumpers, both doing extraordinarily low speeds. A side light had been smashed. The curtains in the bakery tea rooms twitched violently, a tidy lady who had obviously been to the hairdresser that afternoon came out of her perfect tile-hung cottage carrying a cup of tea upon a saucer, followed by a yapping Pekinese. She stood and watched and sipped. A military-looking moustachioed gentleman appeared from nowhere carrying a stiff broom with which he swept up the tiny amount of broken plastic. It was ten minutes before all the spectators withdrew and the spectacle was over.

There is a reedy, dyke-edged lane which leads out at the end of the village down on to the ever-changing and eerie marsh, where there is still remoteness to be found. You can hear lapwings calling and in the spring thousands of 'laughing' frogs. There are twenty-odd churches, some as spectacular as Norfolk's, built on mounds just above the flood level and usually with huge buttresses to support their uncertain footings. The See of Canterbury was the richest landowner on the marsh, which explains the wealth of churches.

Past the potato fields, at Beckets Barn Farmhouse, hangs the huge heavy key to the loneliest church of all – St Thomas à Becket, Fairfield. A causeway over dykes and sheep droppings leads towards it. As I walked a heron flapped over me, alarmingly low, like a small aeroplane. A church has stood here since the thirteenth century, most often approached by boat or, more bravely, by horse – a mounting block still stands outside. Although it was virtually rebuilt in 1913, the inside feels immediately holy and peaceful. The timbers are washed-out oak, almost silver, the Georgian box pews and three-decker pulpit are painted white, and a huge oak beam divides the chancel and nave.

When Richard Ingrams asked the artist John Piper about Romney Marsh (on which he had published a King Penguin in 1950) he said, 'What I really like about it is that it is all – 97 per cent – atmosphere.'

ARBERY'S

Wantage, Berkshire

AFTER THE true loneliness you experience wandering down wide aisles in the Wantage Woolworths, where no one wants to help you and where you are unable to find what you are looking for, it is a relief to cross the market square and enter Arbery's – draper's, hosier's and haberdasher's. Arbery's is a completely unwrecked shop. Here, a host of kindly ladies are longing to help you and make you feel at home.

Wantage is a satisfactory county town: a handsome collection of red-brick and white-stucco houses surround and lead off from the market square; beside the church a footpath leads down to Letcombe Brook between high-walled gardens; Victorian tile-hung and barge-boarded villas abound in its suburbs and the usual plague of mini roundabouts orbit its outskirts, sending the unsuspecting shooting off into new housing estates, dead ends and one-way systems. Until the Great Western Railway struck out across the Vale of the White Horse, the town lay remotely at the foot of the downs and was said to be a sanctuary for thieves who had fled the slum around Westminster Abbey known as 'Alsatia'. It was called 'Black Wantage'. In 1846 the Tractarian Reverend William John Butler became vicar and radically changed the image of the town, founded the famous Wantage Sisterhood and built many fine Victorian buildings. But Wantage's most famous son is King Alfred, who was born in a now lost palace somewhere beside the Letcombe Brook. His statue commands the square where Arbery's flaunts its fine façade, built in the local style of blue-and-red brick. It faces north, of course, like every fine draper should.

There has been a draper's shop here since the beginning of the nineteenth century, but it wasn't until 1894 that Mr John Nicholas

Arbery, a draper from Wellington in Somerset, bought the premises and gave it a fine new front with barley-sugar columns. His son Howard Arbery married a Miss Farnham, the daughter of a clockmaker from Lyme Regis – a Farnham clock still ticks on the mantelpiece in the back room of the shop. 'Close personal attention' was always the Arbery's maxim and it is one which the present John Arbery, who is seventy-eight and still lives above the shop, adheres to exactly a hundred years later.

'In the old days you'd come in the shop knowing exactly what you wanted,' says Mr Arbery. 'Browsers seem to be a new phenomenon. I suppose it's because people have much more time nowadays.' Under the glass-topped counter there are tiered drawers full of cardboard reels of every sort of satin ribbon, blanket binding, knicker elastic and petersham. 'You can buy the lengths you want; you can even buy buttons singly,' says Eileen Barnes, Mr Arbery's sister, who has been serving in the shop since 1931. She remembers when the men used to go out from the yard at the back in pony traps to take orders in all the surrounding villages, at the end of the week they would go round delivering the parcels. She always refers to her brother as 'Mr Arbery'. 'I got told off by a customer for calling him John,' says Mrs Barnes, who still sees the regular reps and does the buying on the ladies' side of things; Mr Arbery buys the men's. The haberdashery suppliers Olney Anson had just gone into liquidation after 150 years. 'It has been a sad day. They are packing up or being taken over all the time. You can't buy brace buttons any more, or woollen combinations,' says Mrs Barnes. 'Perhaps people don't need them; you know, some people don't even wear vests any more.'

Behind the counter is a set of mahogany drawers, containing darning mushrooms, shoe laces and corset laces. Beside the stairs is a brass pneumatic chute, installed in 1920, which propels the money up to the lady doing the accounts on the first floor. The assistants still use it to send up for change; sometimes they just shout up the tube. There are ten part-time ladies who serve – Mr Arbery calls them 'the girls'. Mrs Hunt has been here for thirty-three years; Mrs Cowie has been doing the books for even longer; and Mrs Isles, who has been serving for thirty-four years, says, 'I've enjoyed every minute of it.'

'I think we went forward too quickly over the last fifty years, reflects Mr Arbery. 'Some of the old values will come back. I think this "Back to Basics" business is right.'

ARBURY HALL

Warwickshire

I WENT to Arbury by barge – cutting through the back of Nuneaton on the Coventry Canal past the gardens of terraced houses, full of washing lines and dogs and vegetables; slowly sailing beside gas works, factories and the railway line and on down towards the suburb of Stockingford. The back is the best side of Nuneaton. Two hundred years ago I could have turned off past Worsted Mill towards Arbury, but the canal has long since dried up. So for a brief moment I had to walk the gloomy streets, throbbing with traffic, until I found my Nirvana and the gates to the park of Arbury. Here is an extraordinary pocket of dreaming eighteenth-century England, quite untouched by the gigantic conurbation all around.

Arbury is the only house in Britain with its own private canal system and, though only the vestiges remain, they are enough to stir a sense of wonder and admiration for the remarkable, polished and intelligent man who created it, Sir Roger Newdegate. He read theology at Oxford and became a distinguished antiquary and MP, whose architectural tastes were more avant garde than most of his peers; he also wrote a dissertation on Hannibal's march across the Alps and founded the Newdegate Prize for poetry at Oxford.

Sir Roger's father, Richard Newdegate, had begun a 'boatways' system at Arbury in the early 1700s, by making use of the existing stream which flowed across the estate, so that he could transport timber from his woods to be used in his coal mines at Collycroft. Sir Roger elaborated on this, creating a system comprising five short canals – some now nettle-filled – which cut through his collieries and parks, single, double and triple locks, pools galore, and an underground boat house.

Arbury has belonged to the Newdegates since the sixteenth

century and the original mid-Elizabethan house was built on the site of an Augustinian priory beside the Hall Pond. Around this Sir Roger wrapped a revolutionary-looking house in the middle of the eighteenth century – for my money the best Gothic Revival house in England. It was miles ahead of its time and even better than that swank Sir Horace Walpole's house near Strawberry Hill, the building which lends this particular style its name.

Although several advisers like Sanderson Miller, Henry Keene and Couchman of Warwick were involved in the plans, it is likely that Sir Roger designed much of it himself. The interior of the house is richer and rarer than you could ever imagine – fan-vaulted ceilings covered in a lace of fine plasterwork spring above you; all is light, elegant, inventive and romantic. Sir Roger must have been a romantic himself – he named one of his boats the *Hester Barge*, after his second wife, and loved to take her and parties of friends on long canal trips, returning to graceful Gothic Arbury in the setting sun.

'If only some English Watteau had been there to paint it; the castellated house of grey-tinted stone, with the flickering sunbeams sending dashes of golden light across the many-shaped panes . . .' wrote George Eliot, who used Arbury as her model for Cheverel Manor in her first novel, *Scenes From Clerical Life*. She was born here on the estate to which her father was agent, but later quarrelled with her family, never to return. Her novels tell of remembered places: 'These things make the gamut of joy in landscape to Midland-bred souls – the things they toddled among, or learned by heart, standing between their father's knees, while he drove leisurely . . .' she wrote in *Middlemarch*.

ASHLEWORTH

Gloucestershire

IN THIS little-known and unfashionable corner of Gloucestershire, where the river Severn winds down from Worcestershire among strange hills which rise suddenly like molehills on a lawn, the village of Ashleworth straggles around a green, a quiet mile away from the main Gloucester-to-Ledbury road. It seems an ordinary enough village, and not the sort to attract tourists. The noble golden limestone of the Cotswolds, which outsiders associate with the Gloucestershire villages of their imaginations, has given way to red brick and half timbering. Here begins a flavour of Midlands architecture, with taller houses and black-and-white barns in apple orchards.

Ashleworth's hidden glory lies a quarter of a mile down a tiny road which leads to the great tidal river. Here, beside the quay, is the perfect group of tithe barn, church and house, ancient and unperturbed. Because of their importance at the time of building they are all of stone, which would have been brought up the river by boat. The church of St Andrew and St Bartholomew is predominantly in the Perpendicular style, but contains many other periods, including some herring-bone masonry of about 1100. It is wonderful and captivates you the moment you enter; I can't recommend it too highly. It was well restored in 1869 by the architect Thomas Fulljames, who built himself the fanciful Gothic mansion of Foscombe high on one of the giant molehills outside the village.

Next to the church is Ashleworth Court, a sombre and restrained-looking house which, apart from some minimal outside alterations (it is now tiled instead of thatched), has survived virtually unchanged since it was built in the middle of the fifteenth century. It is rare to find houses this early which have not had radical alterations. The

Court's general demeanour is suitably pious and ecclesiastical and fits its setting to a tee: the antithesis of the flamboyant Elizabethan house which appeared a century later.

The gigantic and magnificent barn completes the great stone trio. It was built during Abbot Newland's time in the late fifteenth and early sixteenth centuries and cannot fail to amaze. Its structure is so simple, powerful and durable. Much of the timber is original and there is no reason to suppose it will not last another 600 years. A barn of this spectacular size and grandeur is, as William Morris justly describes the barn at Great Coxwell, 'As noble as a cathedral'. Unlike the latter, however, the outside of a great barn seldom tells of the extraordinary scale within. Who could not but be awestruck by the sheer height and volume of space?

When Hardy was writing about Bathsheba Everdene's barn in *Far From the Madding Crowd*, he wrote of the functional continuity of such structures compared to castles and churches. 'For once,' he noted, 'medievalism and modernism had a common standpoint. The lanceolate windows, the time-eaten archstones and chamfers, the orientation of axis, the misty chestnut work of the rafters referred to no exploded fortifying art or outworn religious creed. The defence and salvation of the body by daily bread is still a study, a religion, a desire.' Ashleworth Barn was full of pigs and sheep when I went – a tribute to the National Trust, which owns it. A barn's adaptability is endless. At Frocester, south of Gloucester, there is a sensational early fourteenth-century barn of not less than thirteen bays, and it is still as invaluable to its owners today as it has always been over the last seven centuries. It serves at one end as a grain store and at the other as a winter cattle shelter.

I was going to write about the tithe barn in the village of Harmondsworth, two or three stone's throws from Heathrow Airport. It had long been a secret place of mine; my father first took me there twenty years ago. There, stranded as the village is between motorways and runways, was a pocket of untouched rural Middlesex with a pretty flint-and-brick church among great yew trees, and beside it a working farm which just happened to possess the greatest wooden, tile-roofed barn in the country – 190 feet long, 36 feet wide and 36 feet tall.

Last week I took my son to see it. The farmhouses had been converted into 'units' and fine gravel abounded where once there had been mud. The changing of the farm into a business centre had all been done in the 'best possible taste'. It was another country. Discreet English Heritage signs pointed to the beached whale of a barn which, though beautifully restored, was dead. Running to seek solace in the church we found it locked. There was no clue to where the key was and the vicar was not in his vicarage, where groundsel flourished in the flowerbeds. Stick to Ashleworth. It is what Harmondsworth used to be like, unwrecked.

THE AYOTS

Hertfordshire

THERE is a pocket of hidden Hertfordshire, tucked away from Welyn, and sometimes from the madding lorries' drone, in the safety of old Whig estate country. Narrow holly-edged lanes twist this way and that through properly husbanded England. There are trees in the hedgerows, hunting copses, and well-loved woodland where the odd pheasant wanders alone through the undergrowth, not in tame armies bred for the new urban businessman's shoot.

If you are belting up or down the A1, which slices through the countryside like an axe through a loaf of bread, you will never know what glory you are passing unless you leave time to branch off. Take the Lemsford-to-Wheathampstead road. You will very soon get a good square-on view northwards, through the grand, wrought-iron gates of Brocket Hall, set gently down amidst elegant parkland laid out in the 1770s by Richard Wood of Essex. The house was designed by James Paine for Sir Penistone Lamb, later Lord Melbourne, and his father Matthew. Very soon afterwards there is a small sign for Water End on the right; here begins the magical mystery tour.

The lane leads down to the wandering river Lea, where a shallow ford rushes over the road and down a short waterfall towards Hatfield and on to join the Mimram at Hertford. Just above, within sound of the water and set cosily into the rising slope of the hill, stands a beautiful small rose-brick Jacobean manor house. It has three gables, lashings of wisteria and its long side wall gently bulges outwards. It was once the modest home of Sarah Jennings, who married John Churchill, the first Duke of Marlborough.

If you travel on up the lane, which becomes almost a tunnel of steep banks and old nut trees, past a good red-brick farm and black-weatherboarded barn (typical Hertfordshire), you can eventually curl

off to the right for Ayot Green, a peaceful estate village of eighteenth-
and nineteenth-century cottages studded around an arcadian green
where old oak and chestnut trees spread their shade. The place is well
kempt, with only one unforgivable outbreak of cypress leylandii
beside which the road leads down past a fine pair of estate cottages to
the back gates of Brocket Hall.

Ayot St Peter is next, a lovely secret place where, if you try hard
enough, you can make the continuous whine of traffic on the A1
sound like the sea. It is just a hamlet with a distant Jacobean manor
and the most surprising little church of red, white and blue brick,
with a blue mosaic clock face set in its spire and rose windows on its
sides. The door was locked and it was raining when I went with a
church-crawling friend. The notice board on the roadside had a note
pinned up: 'Traditional services using the book of common prayer
every Sunday at 11.15. This church is in danger of being shut down.'
The key was not in the wonderful rose-windowed schoolhouse next
door (by the same architect, Seddon), nor in the large, mid-Victorian
vicarage opposite, but in Welyn. It was too far so we had to be
content with the imagined 'exceptionally complete interior of church
furnishings about 1880 by an architect in sympathy with the then
recent Arts and Crafts tendencies', which Pevsner describes in his
Buildings of England. I know we missed a lot.

At the next village of Ayot St Lawrence we didn't. Narrow
unmarked lanes full of old man's beard brought us to red-brick
cottages with casement windows and leaded panes, the half-timbered
Brocket Arms, the Old Rectory, a red telephone box, and as romantic
an old ruined church as could be, ivy clad and wildly overgrown. Sir
Lionel Lyde, the lord of the manor in the 1770s, decided that the
church spoiled the view from his nearby seat and began to demolish
it while building a new church further away. The Bishop of Lincoln
got to hear of it and an injunction was issued to stop the church being
further despoiled. Nothing was ever done to repair the church and it
still remains much as it was left at the end of the eighteenth century.

Sir Lionel's new church went ahead, set at a good distance from his house so that it caught the eye. To ask the revolutionary Greek Revivalist Charles Revett to design a new church then was as radical a step as asking Richard Rogers to build one today. It is, in effect, a stretched-out and severely simple Greek temple in white stucco. Inside it is sparse and ungodly. Its see-through wings spread out at each side to house the stone pineapple-topped tombs of Sir Lionel at one end and his wife at the other – they were said not to get on.

A mile south is Bride Hall, ancient home of the Parr family, and winding out of the village and out of the spell of the magical Ayots you will come to an undistinguished Victorian house in a dull and disappointing setting. It used to be the vicarage until Sir George Bernard Shaw bought it in 1906 and characteristically re-named it Shaw's Corner. Among other things it contains a hall full of hats, a bicycling machine and a Bechstein piano at which he sat and sang Italian opera to his own accompaniment while the air-raid sirens wailed. In the garden is an ordinary lawnmower shed which he used as a study in the summer. He was a vegetarian and lived here until he died in 1950 at the age of ninety-four.

BARNSBURY

London

An air of modesty reigns over Barnsbury – this leafy half square mile of London, set on a gentle hillside. It is as dignified as it was always meant to be when it was first developed between the 1820s and the 1850s with the swelling middle classes in mind. It was for clerks and small-time merchants who depended on the City for their jobs – people like Dickens's Mr Guppy and Grossmith's Mr Pooter, who in fact lived in Holloway, a neighbouring district. Holborn, gateway to the City, is a mile away. In the nineteenth century, what could have been healthier or more convenient than to live in these exemplary squares and terraces set around new, friendly Gothic churches and the straggling vestiges of an earlier commercial life along the Liverpool Road?

Thornhill began building on his eighty-six acres in 1820 and his first houses fetched £450 each, affording 'fixtures, water closets, cupboards, stoves . . . and three parlours and passages of grained satin wood'. Thomas Milner Gibson developed his acres between 1824 and 1846 and his name lingers in street and square, while the indomitable master builder Mr Cubitt, who later developed Belgravia and Pimlico, joined the band-wagon. In 1827 a sonnet appeared in *Hone's Table Book*:

> You who are anxious for a country seat,
> Pure air, green meadows and suburban views;
> Rooms snug and light – not overlarge but neat,
> And gardens water'd with refreshing dews,
> May find a spot adapted to your taste,
> Near Barnsbury Park, or rather Barnsbury Town,
> Where everything looks elegant and chaste,
> And wealth reposes on a bed of down.

In its day Barnsbury was a riproaring success, but its genteel popularity plummeted after the First World War and its abandoned streets begun to crumble and decay. It was not until the 1960s that the same middle classes started the recolonization of Barnsbury.

The local Labour council, perhaps realizing that Barnsbury was being 'taken over', bought up the odd street and square with a view to redeveloping or rehabilitating them. They pulled down some streets and left barricaded open spaces, but they also refurbished other areas, most notably Milner Square, which offers some of the strangest, most exclusive council housing in London.

The square was designed in 1841 by the architects Roumieu and Gough, who tried to break away from the uniform Regency classicism of the day by elongating everything as though it were elastic. The thin windows between thin pilasters give a ribby effect and make the square look as modern today as it must have looked when it was built. It has become a test case for architectural students to analyse. Sir John Summerson, that most articulate of architectual historians, said that you can visit it many times and 'still not be absolutely certain that you have seen it anywhere but in an unhappy dream'. Simon Jenkins thinks it should have been left on the drawing board and Christopher Hussey, editor of *Country Life*, found it monotonous but impressive.

More conventional is Gibson Square – plain ordinary classical – but within its central garden is a surprising modern temple, designed by our late great architect Raymond Erith to cover a ventilation shaft for the Victoria Line.

Then there is a Lonsdale Square, like a tall Victorian neo-Tudor vicarage multiplied by about forty and set round a square. It was designed by a friend of Pugin, and no friend of Pugin's could possibly build in the classical idiom. Gothic was the *only* architecture to be contemplated – down with the Greek gods and back to our own cosy medievalism. I've never seen a square like this anywhere.

Barnsbury is stock and stucco all over: either its houses are of the greyish-yellowish London stock brick, or painted white stucco, or a mixture of both. This general uniformity does not mean there are not extraordinary surprises. On the gentle rise of Richmond Avenue, behind the plane trees you suddenly find yourself in Egypt. Sphinxes guard the doors and Tutankhamun-like decorations adorn the houses. There is regular gospel singing in the Celestial Church of Christ in Cloudesley Square and in the middle of Thornhill Square there is the best display I have ever seen of yellow, apricot and orange shrub roses, with standards rising above the packed beds.

At the west end of Thornhill Square stands a sensational striped red-and-yellow brick library designed by Beresford Pyte in 1906. Over each of its windows is a decorated letter of the alphabet. An awful plastic 'WEST LIBRARY' logo sign demeans it. I am told that local residents are fighting to keep it open.

Apart from Barnsbury's endlessly unfolding delights, like the Albion pub and the Edwardian flats in Thornhill Road, the all-pervading and extraordinary thing about it is the quiet. In the early sixties David Wagner, a resident and a town planner, put forward a proposal to keep Barnsbury's 'village' character by excluding major traffic from its centre. By 1970 it had become London's first major experiment in traffic management. It is now a maze of blocked-off street entrances laced with sleeping policemen, which serve to infuriate passing drivers and delight its inmates. You *have* to walk in Barnsbury and that cannot fail to make you happy.

BOOTON

Norfolk

NEAR the small, mellow-brick town of Reepham, along a dipping, well-hedged lane, straggles the strange and little-known hamlet of Booton – a sparse scattering of houses around a much-pinnacled and wildly eccentric church, the creation of the Reverend Whitwell Elwin. If you look northwards towards the coast you get a spectacular view of the most beautiful churches in Norfolk – Salle, the largest of 659, and Cawston. Their great towers rise majestically from this mild and gentle East Anglian landscape; Salle's from huge, lonely arable fields, and the fourteenth-century Cawston's from the huddling roofs of a little town. Perhaps it was their inspirational glory in this particularly pretty bit of the county which led Whitwell Elwin to Booton, coupled with the fact that his uncle, Caleb Elwin, was already patron and rector there in the 1830s when Whitwell decided to take holy orders.

Booton's houses and church evoke a vignette of Victorian ecclesiastical life, centring round the magnetic character of its incumbent. Whitwell Elwin was a direct descendant of Pocahontas, the Native American princess who married an Englishman and died at Gravesend, and his profile bore witness to this. He came from a long line of parsons, lawyers and soldiers. He was destined for the law, but after falling in love with and marrying his cousin in 1834 he decided that it would be more secure to go into the clergy.

He took to heart the words of Bishop Law at his ordination a few years later: 'I was once a country parson as you will now be, but in an evil hour I was tempted to take the office of a bishop and have been a miserable man ever since. Now take my advice, never accept preferments; remain as you are and you will be happy.'

Whitwell followed his advice to the letter, and although he was

Above: Bailey gate, Castle Acre.

Above: The chute at Arbery's.

Above: The Grand Military Canal, Appledore.

Top left: Arbury Hall.

Bottom left: The tithe barn, Ashleworth.

Right: Ayot St Lawrence's church.

Below: Neo-Egyptian in Barnsbury.

Left: Church of St Michael the Archangel, Booton.

Top right: Brympton d'Evercy.

Bottom right: Church of St Mary the Virgin, Cartmel.

Below: Cottage on the green at Breamore.

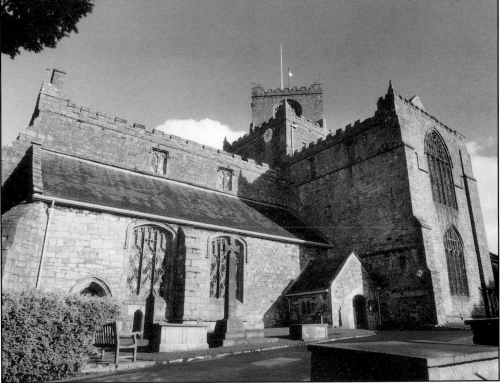

Above: Above Little Harp Bay, Clevedon.

Left: Goldney Grotto, Clifton.

Top right: Clovelly.

Bottom right: Clun Castle.

Above: Church of St Swithun's, Compton Beauchamp.

Above: Dorney Court.

Left: Edensor.

offered preferment in later life, he declined and stayed in Booton. One of the first things he did was to build a solid rectory to the west of the church, which was paid for by his wife's dowry. In true Evangelical style it was never decorated; the family had no carpets, curtains or heating, but it was filled to the brim with books. Elwin found it impossible to bridle his energy and content himself with being just a country parson and, after contributing some brilliant articles to the influential *Quarterly Review*, he eventually became its editor. So large was the volume of correspondence he generated, a letter box had to be installed in Booton.

Elwin's literary friends were numerous and included Thackeray, who called him 'Dr Primrose'; but perhaps more important to him were the young females in his his life, his 'blessed girls', for he had a passion for developing young people's minds and characters. One of these was Emily Lytton, to whom he became an intimate friend and counsellor. When their friendship began she was thirteen and he seventy, and their ensuing correspondence was published much later by Emily, who married the architect Edwin Lutyens. She described his 'remarkable understanding and sympathy'.

Another of his long-standing 'blessed girls' was Eliza Holley, the daughter of a local solicitor, who as a young girl felt lonely and sorry for herself. Elwin brought a new element to her life and she retained an almost dog-like devotion to him. She never married and in 1879, on inheriting her share of the family fortune amassed from selling land to the railways, she asked Elwin to design her a house near his church. It is now called Hollies House, and stands on the crossroads. Although Elwin and his friends tried to persuade her to build the house further back from the road and the then green lane, she was determined to have it as close as possible to the two thoroughfares.

As soon as it was habitable she moved into the attics and never bothered to finish the bottom two floors. The servants had to carry everything up from the kitchen. The front staircase was never finished, but stopped halfway, leaving a dangerous gap on the upstairs landing. In the end there was a fatal accident when a maidservant stepped into the gap in the dark. A barrier was then erected.

Perhaps because of the death of three of his five children, Elwin began to harness his restless energy into building the church of St Michael the Archangel to replace the existing one. He was then fifty years old, had trained neither as an architect nor a draughtsman, and relied on explaining his ideas to local builders, who then interpreted them in their own fashion.

Elwin had visited myriad churches and cathedrals, many in the company of the ever-faithful Miss Holley, and it was her money – £1,500 a year for twenty years – which subsidized the extraordinary fantasy which stands today. Many of the features of its design are taken from, for instance, Lichfield Cathedral, Temple Balsall in Warwickshire, St Stephen's Chapel at Westminster and Glastonbury Abbey. The 'blessed girls' are supposedly represented in the huge flying angels in the roof.

Booton's religious leanings may have changed, but its appearance has not. The Lutyens-designed Booth Manor, built for a member of the Elwin family, lurks enticingly down a tree-lined drive; Hollies House is alive with inventive members of the Fry family. The rectory, where the last rector, Willis Feast, gave huge teas and brought up eight children, is sold; the church is now looked after by that admirable organization, the Churches Conservation Trust (formerly the Redundant Churches Fund).

BREAMORE

Hampshire

BREAMORE is the most beautiful place. It is in the Hampshire of wide valleys between chalk downs where villages cluster along river banks and where houses are of rose-red brick and churches of dressed flint. Breamore village itself is startlingly picturesque and must be as unwrecked as any in the south of England. This is largely because the whole village was always owned by one family who, until quite recently, decided upon its losses and additions and whose totalitarian but informed aesthetic decisions have made for unadulterated beauty. Breamore (pronounced Bremmer) is now a protected area.

One half of the village clings to the river Avon and the relentless Salisbury-to-Bournemouth road. The other half, the most beautiful one, is scattered artfully around the great wide marsh, where bent willows shade grazing cattle and occasional flocks of geese. The marsh is common to all tenants and is unfenced but for the occasional single strand of electric wire. It looks settled and timeless with ravishing, half-hidden eighteenth and nineteenth century thatched cottages around its edges. The village is not set in picturesque concrete, like Laycock, for instance, where you are hardly allowed to put your dustbins out for fear of detracting from the 'olde worlde' picture. Breamore has had many changes in the past and is still changing today, but it happens, in most cases, gently and unobtrusively.

Upper Street straggles further towards the downs and is shaded by evergreen oaks and a giant sycamore at Cross Trees corner, beside which is a rare and genuine cottage garden. The flower-lined path here leads up a slight incline to the best cottage in the village. It has been quietly repaired over the years and has had no tarting up whatsoever, whereas its semi-detached neighbour has had the inevitable young marrieds' over-enthusiastic fast-track 'renovation' treatment, with a drive-in for the car, and a consequent loss of unselfconscious beauty. Towards the west of the 'upper' village there are some good brick farm buildings with carthorse-harness hooks still in place and a grand little doctor's house with very satisfactory railings and gate piers set, perfectly symmetrically, in a low brick wall.

A little way from the upper half of Breamore village is the best Saxon church in Hampshire, built of whole flints with simple stone dressings around the doors and windows. With its small squat bellcote, the church is high and huddled and strange. Over the archway to the south transept is an Anglo-Saxon inscription which translates as: 'Here the Covenant becomes manifest to thee.' The church stands curtained by yews on the edge of a cedar-dotted park where a mellow red-brick Elizabethan manor house looks out to the distant woods of the New Forest on the horizon.

The house was completed in 1593 and because of its crisp perfection one is tempted to think it is Victorian. The poor ill-fated family of Dodingtons who built it and lived here had an awful time. William Dodington, in anxiety over a suit pending in the Star Chamber, 'went up St Sepulchre's Steeple, threw himself over the battlements and broke his neck'. This suicide in broad daylight on the 11 April 1600 caused a considerable sensation. The portrait of his wife Christian hangs in the great hall. As if this was not enough, their son William's wife was murdered by their son Henry in Breamore House itself. The house and much of the estate were sold in the eighteenth century to Sir Edward Hulse, whose descendants live here today.

It is worth every step of the mile-and-a-half walk through wonderful woods to reach the mysterious Mizmaze – an 85-foot-wide labyrinth cut into the turf – set in one of the best bits of downland left in the south of England. At a 'crossroads' of the tracks right in the middle of the wood there is a fine old tree with a divided trunk, known to generations of Breamore children as 'Twin Oak'. As you emerge from the wood you see before you an unspoilt tract of downland on whose crest is a copse of yew and nut trees which hides the Mizmaze. Nobody knows how old it is; perhaps its origins are connected with the twelfth-century Breamore Priory. There are little over a dozen such mazes left in England, but in medieval times there were 1,000 across the country. Its pattern is much like many of the labyrinths found on the floors of great cathedrals all over Europe. As with the white horses of the chalk uplands, the Mizmaze needs regular weeding to keep it from becoming covered in grass and brambles. This job was traditionally done by local villagers. A few years ago it had to be almost totally re-made after a gang of motorcyclists were said to have driven all over it and cut it to ribbons. Since then Mr Hulse has been instructed by the ancient monument authorities to surround it, like poor Stonehenge, with a fence.

BRYMPTON D'EVERCY

Somerset

YEOVIL never claimed to be a beauty. Although it suffered a disastrous fire in the fifteenth century, the town's spirit remained undaunted and it fast became a centre for the leather trade. It is now the home of Westland Helicopters. Though Edward Hutton, writing in *Highways and Byways in Somerset* at the beginning of the century, called Yeovil 'the most disappointing town in Somerset', he goes on to say, 'the traveller must console himself with the knowledge that Yeovil is the key to that district of Somerset, which is perhaps richest in beautiful and ancient villages . . .' In nearby Preston Plucknett a medieval manor stands beside a magnificent tithe barn. Further along is Montacute, that awe-inspiring pin-up of an Elizabethan house. But best of all, and best in all Someset for my money, is the magical group of buildings at Brympton d'Evercy.

Brympton is a secret place in a lost pocket of farmland on the outskirts of the town. If you approach it by car you are channelled through Yeovil's bright trading estate where the curb stones are fresh as daisies and neo-Japanese superstores abound. Then, as suddenly as this American sprawl began, so it ends in unadulterated Somerset. A hawthorn-hedged lane leads to a seventeenth-century thatched farmhouse surrounded by straggling stone buildings. Before it, the short drive to Brympton begins, leading round a steep bend to this unexpected glory. Swathes of lawn backed by flowerbeds and balustrades herald this most perfect of English scenes – the beautiful Tudor façade of the manor house, the thirteenth-century chantry house to the south, and beside it the parish church of St Andrew. To the north, completing a courtyard effect, is the 1730 clock tower and a little further back an early eighteenth-century stable block.

Although the buildings vary in date, they are all of the same bright golden Ham stone, quarried from Ham hill, a few miles west. The effect is utterly harmonious, and the weathered stone is speckled with pale-gold and grey lichen. Each time I visit Brympton I am bowled over by its beauty; it stokes up my spirit like nowhere else I know. I am by no means alone. The late Christopher Hussey was constantly being asked which was the most beautiful place he had ever seen. He wrote:

> Nearly every country-house has some quality about it whether of architecture, sentiment, historical associations or scenery that makes it, in the narrower sense of the word, incomparable. But Brympton has them all and unites them so perfectly that the whole cannot be surpassed. There are greater, more historic, more architecturally impressive buildings in grander scenery; but I know of none of which the whole impression is more lovely. None that summarizes so exquisitely English country life.

Few documents record the building of Brympton, but it is known that the d'Evercy family bought the land in the thirteenth century. The chantry house could possibly have been part of an original manor and over the next two centuries the d'Evercys built and added to their home.

Brympton then passed to the Sydenham family. In the 1670s John P. Sydenham built on the most beautiful south-facing wing imaginable. It may be a puzzle to academics, who cannot decide when it was built, but it certainly satisfies the soul of us non-experts. How could anything be more lovely? Before the wing there is a wide gravel walk which looks out over a balustrade to a small lake and the gentle slopes of lush cattle-strewn pasture beyond. A faint hum of traffic wafts across from Yeovil but the atmosphere of Brympton is protective, the ivy-clad, brick walled gardens all-encompassing.

The fourteenth-century church – perhaps luckily – saw no rich inhabitants during the last century and so escaped any tarting up. The Sydenhams were broke by the early 1700s and in 1731 Francis Fane bought Brympton. A colourful Victorian inheritor through the female line was Sir Spencer Ponsonby, a nephew of Lady Georgina Fane, who was a co-founder of the I Zingari Cricket Club and began a strong tradition of cricket which is still upheld today on the field below the lake.

CARTMEL

Lancashire

CARTMEL is probably the least-known National Hunt racecourse in England and also the most beautiful. It is a place for sellers, amateur riders and novice hurdlers – but then it is out on a limb, albeit a ravishing one at the foot of the Lake District, where the mountains have turned into friendlier hills and the smell of the sea is on the air.

Racing has long been in Cartmel's blood, perhaps orginated by bored medival monks from the priory who were said to race their mules along the sands on their way to Lancaster across Morecambe Bay. The track undulates unnervingly in this beautiful bit of north Lancashire, the chosen site of the ancient British camp. It is only a mile round, so nobody needs binoculars. It is either visible to the naked eye or obscured altogether when it travels through trees – more like a point-to-point course than a racecourse, sometimes getting very narrow, and at one point flanked by a solid lakeland stone wall.

Being so tucked away it isn't surprising that one of racing's most brilliant coups took place in Cartmel in 1974, when Gay Future came in at 10 to 1 at the August Bank Holiday meeting. Thought to be trained by an unknown Scottish permit holder named Collins and ridden by an unknown Irish jockey, the horse had in fact been switched at the last moment three miles from the track and was ridden by a top Irish amateur. It's a longer story than that, but the upshot was that the Irish betting team who were hitting every betting-shop in London weren't paid, although in fact the coup was, in my book, legitimate. Scotland Yard was called in and winning payouts were withheld. It was by no means the first time that the bookies had been outwitted over a Cartmel race, but it was the first time the police were involved, and a national scandal ensued.

Cartmel village could hardly be bettered; it is just as Ward Lock and Co.'s *Red Guide* described it at the beginning of the century: 'A quiet place, a cathedral city in miniature, happy in the possession of a fine old priory church, one of the few which escaped the destruction at the dissolution.' This great cathedral-like church, which dominates the village, is part of the vanished priory founded by William Marshall, Earl of Pembroke, towards the end of the twelfth century. Because it was also designed as the parish church for the local community of cocklers and fishermen at the outset, it was allowed to remain intact when all else was destroyed. The choir stalls and screens are exceptional and in the vestry is one of the earliest umbrellas in existence, with a leather canopy. The church also owns a first edition of Spenser's *Faerie Queene*.

There is a good five-bayed early eighteenth-century house near the church, of the calibre you'd expect to find in a cathedral close, and pretty seventeenth- and eighteenth-century cottages line the winding streets and the brook which runs through the village. There are now also three gift shops, three antique shops, a needlework shop, and two very good second-hand bookshops. Mr Baines-Smith's in the square has one of the best collections of children's books in the North of England – *Biggles*, *Just William*, Arthur Ransome and, not unnaturally, Beatrix Potter. Mr Kerr started his bookshop at the bottom of the fourteenth-century gatehouse in 1933, in the still-unchanged premises of a Victorian draper's shop: he specializes in 'railwayana'. What nicer station to call your own than Grange-over-Sands just down the road?

Stand in Cartmel's central square and the views are lovely in all directions. The whole place is picturesque without being overdone. There are good pubs – the Cavendish Arms, the King's Arms and the Royal Oak – and Tom and Di Peter, who worked at the Miller Howe for thirteen years and learned under the famous chef John Tovey, run Upland, an airy, pleasant Edwardian hotel a mile out of Cartmel. It's worth saving up for.

Racing is on summer and spring Bank Holidays, when there is a funfair. The crowds are usually enormous. The Cavendishes' home, Holker Hall (pronounced 'Hooker' by some and 'Hole-ker' by Lancastrians), is close by and well worth a visit – a great red sandstone pile, predominantly Victorian, set in an almost unbeatable park.

CLEVEDON

Somerset

CLEVEDON is classy. It stands high above and aloof from the humdrum neighbouring resort of Weston-Super-Mare, and apart from its upstream and workmanlike neighbours, Portishead and Avonmouth. It retains a reserved dignity, turning its face to distant hills and attracting a *recherché* type of commuter. Many a renowned doctor and orthodontist drives homeward in the evening across Clifton suspension bridge from the city of Bristol along the line of hills to Clevedon.

If you have ever seen the sign to Clevedon from the M5 motorway as you whisk down to the West Country, this strange sliver between the heavy hum of traffic and the mouth of the great river Severn looks almost inaccessible and the resort itself irresistible, half hidden and huddled as it is behind a wall of hill and cliff.

Clevedon is twelve miles from Bristol across deep wooded gorge-y country. If you follow the road along Tickenham Hill, Court Hill and The Warren, the town begins to reveal itself and unfurl around corners – it seems like an ordinary enough place, not at all to do with the sea among these hills and valleys. Then suddenly and unexpectedly you are out on the blustery estuary where the Scots pines are trained into a horizontal position by the wind and the air wafts salt. To stand on the path above Little Harp Bay with a low wall between you and the water is exactly like being on the deck of a liner – when the tide is high it races by at such a speed that you feel you are moving along. You look out across the ruffled water, muddy after a March storm, to Wales, which seems no distance away. Newport is directly opposite and beyond it rise the hills, often covered in snow in winter.

The air of Clevedon is mild and invigorating, free from sudden changes,' reads the 1949 official guide to this, 'the Gem of sunny Somerset'. It goes on, 'Fogs are rare while snow is an unusual visitant. The rainfall is curtailed by the influence of the Mendip Hills. Proof of the dryness of the climate is found in the fact that the average local rainfall is considerably less than the average for the eighty-five recording stations in Somerset.' The huge Mendips, in whose midst stands the rock about which Toplady wrote the hymn 'Rock of Ages', do indeed shield the town.

Clevedon began to evolve from a small fishing village into a fashionable resort with the late Georgians, but it didn't really take off until the middle of the nineteenth-century. In the centre of the seafront there are handsome houses with Regency names such as Adelaide House, Brunswick House and Clarence House, and a restaurant called Il Giordino where you can eat lobster. Then northwards and upwards as the cliff rises up the architecture changes and the solidity of Victorian building begins, with sedate villas of the local grey stone in all kinds of styles from Italian to Gothic, though occasionally Regency houses still spring up, particularly in Marine Hill and Hill Road. From Clevedon's heights you can look right down to the Quantocks in deep Somerset.

The pier, undoubtedly the most graceful in the country, was built in the late 1860s. Part of it collapsed under test loading in 1970. It has since undergone a long and worthwhile restoration instigated by indefatigable enthusiasts and helped by English Heritage. Clevedon Pier now ventures out like a daddy long-legs towards Wales and, when the tide is low, is revealed in all its glory awaiting the pavilion which once graced its seaward end. The Clevedon Pier Trust seeks another £250,000 to finish it.

The old parish church of St Andrew, the saint of seamen, is worth a decco; it stands on Clevedon Point, not far from the edge of the cliff but high enough to feel safe from the waves when the wind sets in strong from the west. Apart from climbing Court Hill, from where you can see for ever, to get the best view of Clevedon you can walk along the seafront esplanade from the pier, passing the bandstand

and Little Harp Bay. You then go on by Salthouse Fields up the path through Salthouse Woods to Old Church Hill and then by Poet's Walk round Wayne's Hill, from where there is a wonderful panorama.

Clevedon owes much of its popularity to the Elton family of Clevedon Court, a wonderful ancient manor house set under thick woods just outside the town. It was bought in 1709 by Abraham Elton, a rich Bristol merchant, whose descendants proved to be dedicated and intelligent and went on to be members of Parliament, inventors, writers and patrons of the arts. Lamb, Landor, Tennyson and Thackeray all stayed here. Sir Arthur Elton, a pioneer of the documentary film, left it to the National Trust in 1961. The gardens rise behind the Court in three walled terraces adorned with fountains and borders, until they meet the woods above.

CLIFTON

Bristol

CLIFTON is technically a suburb of Bristol, but in spirit it is worlds apart, a separate place entirely. Although its hey day was in the 1890s it still feels slightly rarefied. In the eighteenth century Clifton made an effort to become a second Bath, and there are terraces and crescents to show for it, as well as exquisite Regency houses of outstanding quality. It may have failed as a spa, but it was always a fashionable place to live.

High on the downs, above the deep gorge spanned by Brunel's suspension bridge, Clifton remains a special treat to visit. The Zoological Gardens are my favourite in England, compact, full of good buildings, stunning flowers and reasonably contented animals. In the sacred close of Clifton College, which rose to fame in the 1860s, the 'breathless hush' was immortalized by Henry Newbolt.

For a time, Clifton was known as the Simla of Bristol and a dainty atmosphere pervaded. A 1950s guidebook described how 'on the Downs there is a liberal sprinkling of ex-Indian Army officers, elderly spinsters and widows eking out their limited capital and reading books from the circulating libraries, and prim schoolmistresses with their young charges tripping in echelons along the white roads or running beneath the lime, ilex and plane trees'. Barbara Pym fitted in beautifully when she shared a house called The Coppice with a group of friends who worked for the BBC during the war. 'And it is Spring again,' she wrote in her diary in April 1942, 'and I have noticed almond trees and forsythia blossom in Clifton as in north Oxford, and the clear evening light comes into the house and one can pick daffodils in the garden.'

Today Clifton, if no longer a haven for ex-colonials, retains a bookish and intellectual atmosphere – BBC officials, university lecturers schoolteachers and students abound. A few female students are lucky enough to live in one of Clifton's best surprises, Goldney House, which now belongs to Bristol University. The garden is one of the most exciting in the country. Perched high on these once-verdant heights, it is a veritable acropolis. Its southern terrace falls away precipitously into the gorge of the river Avon and commands a spectacular view across the city of Bristol below and beyond. This bastion of eighteenth-century taste is hemmed in by steep, winding streets of Georgian, Regency and Victorian houses, and remains a bright jewel in Bristol's crown.

The garden and its star attraction, the grotto, were the work of Thomas Goldney III. His father and grandfather had built up a thriving shipping concern – built up through sponsoring privateering voyages, which must have pricked their Quaker consciences. They were also partners in the Coalbrookdale Ironworks. Thomas III expanded the family business and became a managing director of one of the first partnership banks in Bristol.

By the 1730s he was rich enough to indulge his grand passion for gardening. The Picturesque movement, obsessed with antiquity and romance, was just beginning to burgeon out of the ashes of rigid formality in garden design. Thomas set about expanding his estate and began digging the subterranean passages for his grotto before he had even formally bought the land, but it still took twenty-seven years to complete this sensational 'Aladdin's cave'.

You enter the grotto down a dark tunnel lined in clinker, and on turning a corner see a marble lion and lioness set in a den of grotesquely cut limestone. Further on there is the sound of rushing water cascading down from an urn held by a statue of the reclining Neptune set high among arches and swirling encrustations of crystals, tufa, minerals and shells.

'The bright stillness of the figure is a long way from Bristol,' writes Barbara Jones in her great tome *Follies and Grottoes*, 'and this surely is what a grotto is for, the invocation of a new world . . . the life of the city is petrified, and half a million people and their domestic cats have become Neptune and his lions. Ultimately, Goldney is terrifying . . .'

There are different exits lined in clinker through which to escape if you *have* been frightened. Above ground you will find a baroque statue of a gigantic Hercules; an early Georgian orangery, re-faced in the thirties, in front of a small canal; and a Gothic tower which houses what Goldney referred to as his 'fire engine' but which in fact is a pump which brings the water for the grotto up from a well. Clifton is full of hidden glories and Goldney's grotto is but one of them.

CLOVELLY

Devon

CLOVELLY is one of the most famous villages in England – its picturesqueness beggars belief. But despite the fact that it has around 300,000 visitors a year it remains unwrecked. It is privately owned and retains a faintly unkempt magic that no institutionally owned property would dare display.

On the main road between Bideford and Bude stands an indicator of the quality to come – the Clovelly petrol station. It is handsome, solid, discreet and practical and was designed by a local architect in the early 1930s under the direction of Christine Hamlyn. Much of its splendour has been diminished by a mini-roundabout in front of it, chock-a-block with council clutter and as ugly as could be. Here you turn off on a side road and begin to sail down the hill, past a sawn-off rowing boat upended and made into a cottage garden arbour, towards the high brick gateposts heralding Clovelly Court and church. An Arts and Crafts lodge has emblazoned on its façade, 'Go North, Go South, Go East, Go West, Home is Best' – the maxim of Clovelly's great saviour and benefactress, Christine Hamlyn, who owned the estate and village for fifty-two years and was largely responsible for its present glory.

The short drive arched with lime trees reveals at its end a sylvan park suspended above the sea – scatterings of trees tumble down towards soft undulating woods smothering the high cliffs' edge. All that remains of Clovelly Court after two fires is the original eighteenth-century house, built in the romantic style with towers at its corners and looking Scottishly gaunt and tall. Arches of the local purplish lichen-covered stone link the Court to the church, which has a stunning zigzagged Norman door; the graveyard has more stones packed into it than I've seen in my life. (Charles Kingsley's father was here for a few years.) Beside it is the great secret garden of the Court, enclosed by walls 20 feet high, with doorways of faded blue paint giving glimpses of huge clumps of day lilies and apple trees. The place has a familiar quality that makes you reluctant to leave.

On you go down the winding road, falling precipitously to the village itself, for which Castle Combe, Laycock and Bourton-on-the-Water must wait in the wings. Buses and cars are left on a plateau out of sight next to the clear, simple and exemplary visitors' centre which was built in 1987 and designed by the architect Birkin Haward by way of a limited competition.

A river, now underground, once slithered and waterfalled down the same course as the cobbled street of upended beach pebbles, which leads you down through lush, ferny woods to the quay half a mile below. The village was once a small herring community huddled around the only safe port of call between Westward Ho! and Bude. Hemmed in by the sheer, relentless red-sandstone cliffs which dominate this coastline, the village could only grow upwards. Its cottages cling precariously to the cliffside and each other. By the beginning of the last century there were nearly a thousand inhabitants. The village, which had grown under the auspices of the Hamlyn family, was restored and enhanced by Christine during the first third of this century.

The whitewashed houses and cottages abound with the vestiges of wild and wacky Victorian taste for the romantic and picturesque – wooden and iron balconies, decorative barge-boards, overhanging porches, dormer windows, leaded lights, even some applied *Oberammergau* carving which Christine Hamlyn spied on an opera set. The entire village literally drips with flower – nasturtiums, lobelia, petunias, alyssum, cosmos, geraniums, fuschias, pinks, carnations, begonias and stocks pour out of window boxes, hanging baskets and lobster pots. Roses, honeysuckle and clematis clamber up walls.

Every front garden or bed is crammed with giant flowers – hollyhocks, delphiniums, lupins and arum lilies – which grow twice their normal size in this warm, wet, sheltered fold in the cliffs. Buddleia grows from the chimney pots and ferns from crevices in the walls of beach stone. A cottage advertising bed and breakfast has willow-pattern china laid out on a lace tablecloth behind net curtains. Side alleys wind this way and that, some stepped and leading to narrower streets . . . 'It is a working village – tenancies have to be full-time so that the place doesn't die,' says Mr Rous, Christine Hamlyn's great-nephew, who runs the estate and loves it as she did.

The steep slopes all around are thickly wooded as a result of enlightened planting in the early nineteenth century. Mount Pleasant, a viewing point hanging over the south-west woods, is now owned by the National Trust. A three-mile drive called The Hobby, landscaped by Sir James Hamlyn in 1829, winds eastwards. Hidden by trees are the remains of Dingle Hole, a bat- and spider-filled cavern which leads down and down to a cave on the shore where, in the eighteenth century, a family of forty-eight cannibals called Gregg lived and terrorized the region. Locals say they robbed, murdered and ate a thousand people before being eventually hunted down by 400 men and a pack of bloodhounds.

CLUN

Shropshire

CLUN is a small town of grim grey stone at which I arrived by a switchback of a road that wound endlessly on and on. It has a strong, dour atmosphere, set as it is among 'bare and enormous brown hills all full of bilberries and earthworks' (the *Shell Guide*'s description).

These hills reek of history, for the landscape has been little changed by modern farming – fields are still tree-scattered and there are oak and beech woods hanging on to steep hillsides. Clun itself sits on the convergence of eight roads and was for centuries a fierce bastion protecting the Salopians against the turbulent Welsh.

The castle was one of those sturdy borderland fortresses built by the Normans on top of earlier foundations, the remains of which stand high on a mound to the west of the town in a perfect defensive position, with the river Clun sweeping in a great bow around them. If you stand under the half-ruined tower it is like looking up at a modern skyscraper. During the 1990 Clun earthquake, described by a local as 'being shaken like a rat by a terrier', the castle's tower stood firm as a rock. The pastoral surroundings are often grazed by a flock of dark-faced Clun sheep. English Heritage, who look after the castle, keep it in the romantic and unsanitized state it deserves.

There is a wonderful humpback bridge over the river with five unequal arches and triangular stand-ins into which you can shrink from passing traffic. The present bridge is fourteenth century but its foundation are sixth century, or possibly Roman. The layers of building on top tell of how important this crossing and hence the town was. The local saying, 'Whoever crosses Clun Bridge comes back sharper than he went', is still much quoted, so if you do take these steps you might be described as 'pert as a spoon' in Clun dialect, meaning sharp and bright.

Other good Clun dialect words include 'taxy-waxy' for tough, stringy meat, to 'kwank', meaning to snub, a 'crod' for a short, stocky person, a 'butty' for a comrade or one of a pair (e.g. the left shoe is butty to the right one), and a 'box-neck' for a somersault. The traditional calls for animals include 'hope hope' for cattle, 'ba-hope ba-hope' for sheep, 'wid wid' for ducks, 'gus gus' for geese and 'eya eya' for dogs. Because of its remoteness, Clun's hundreds of strange words are kept alive and well by the locals, mercifully safe from the executive-style euro-waffle which has done so much to ruin and standardize our language. The late Mrs Hamer, from an old Clun farming family who have lived for centuries in an ancient farmhouse at Bicton, did much to safeguard Clun's history by collecting the words in a booklet which you can buy locally.

On the far side of the river from the castle, up a sharp ascent, stands the solid Norman church with its square, fortress-like west tower, which suits the landscape around. There are angels carved on the north aisle roof and Welsh names on the gravestones among the yew trees in the graveyard. Beside the church is a good early-eighteenth-century vicarage, and back across the river again a simple rustic Georgian town hall. Perhaps the town's *pièce de résistance* is the magnificent Hospital of the Holy and Undivided Trinity, a refuge founded by Henry, Earl of Northampton, in 1614 for 'twelve poor men with a warden, sub warden, a nurse and a barber'.

Since prehistoric times Clun has stood on a trade route which crossed the great bare hills. A brilliant and obscure museum contains thousands of arrow-heads found here. In the last century there were fourteen different pubs in Clun which were 'sniving' (swarming) with people on market day. By the 1920s there were eight and now there are only three. The Buffalo remains an old traditional pub; Sir Walter Scott stayed here to get a feel for the place when he was writing *The Betrothed*, in which Clun Castle appears as La Garde Doloreuse.

The adjective in the following old couplet can be changed depending on how you feel:

> Clunton and Clunbury, Clungunford and Clun
> Are the quietest places under the sun

Today, Clun's quietude attracts artists and writers. There is no more than the average contingent of besandalled lettuce-lunchers – enough, however, to produce a fly-sheet which publishes articles with titles such as, 'I saw the Holy Grail on Clun Hill'.

COMPTON BEAUCHAMP

Faringdon, Berkshire

HERE is a secret haven, tucked right under the great chalk Berkshire Downs. Few visit Compton Beauchamp, or know what they are missing. If you approach it across the flat, winding and willowed road from the military town of Shrivenham, past Ruffinswick and then Compton Marsh Farm, the downs grow ever larger as you approach until they seem like mountains. The tiny village consists of little more than a few cottages, a rectory, church and manor house which, if you blink, you miss.

A short lime avenue on a bend in the roads leads your eye to one of the loveliest small country houses in England, 'a gem privily set in a bosky lap of the bare chalk downs . . . a pearl of price combining in high degree amenity of position and charm of layout', wrote Avray Tipping in *Country Life* eighty years ago. The pale limestone façade it presents to the passer-by is devastatingly glamorous and designed to impress. It was not just the house, however, which impressed the many young men who passed it in the 1730s and 40s, but its owner, Ann Richards, who was extremely rich and beautiful, entertained generously but seemed impervious to any advances. She refused suitors one after the other even though, just out of sight of the house, they replaced their riding wigs with their best peruques. The drive is still known as 'Wig Avenue'.

Ann Richards preferred coursing to men. Every day she would take a carriage and six up the steep track behind her house which led across the Ridgeway, past the chambered barrow called Wayland's Smithy and on to a huge tract of open land above Ashdown House. Here she would course hares with her famously fast greyhounds, then return to Compton Beauchamp, where the hounds were given pride of place. When she hired cooks her first question was, 'Young woman, do you love dogs? If you are disposed to stay with me, remember their place in my house is wherever they think fit to go.' She died single in 1771, having written her own epitaph:

> . . . All arts and sciences beside
> This hare-brained heroine did deride.
> An utter foe to wedlock's noose,
> When poaching men had stopt the Meuse.
> Tattle and tea, she was above it,
> And but for form appeared to love it.
> At books she laughed, at Pope and Clarke,
> And all her joy was Ashdown Park.
> But Ann at length was spied by Death,
> Who coursed, and ran her out of breath. . .

Chalk-white St Swithun's church, hidden beside the manor house, is inspiring. It also feels well cared for. There is even a chintz-covered cushion on the cold stone seat in the entrance porch, above which hangs a watercolour of the church dated 1911. The inside appears and feels like untouched medieval but nearly all the furnishings were created through the vision of the well-heeled Anglo-Catholic eccentric Samuel Gurney, who moved into the Victorian rectory in the 1920s. Over a period of twenty years he commissioned the church decorator Martin Travers to enrich the interior, and took terrific trouble in overseeing every detail.

The medieval-looking painting of vines winding wildly all over the thirteenth-century chancel was carried out by Lydia Lawrence, a niece of Judge Bacon, who lived at the manor house in the early 1900s. She was a member of the Kyrle Society, whose object was to 'Brighten the lives of the People' by decorating buildings and planting flowers in cottage gardens. The society was founded in 1877 by Octavia and Victoria Hill in memory of John Kyrle, a celebrated seventeenth-century philanthropist from Ross-on-Wye who gave away hundreds of pounds a year to locals to plant trees and decorate and enhance their houses and gardens.

DORNEY COURT

Buckinghamshire

LEAVING Windsor Castle rising high behind you, you can wend
your way out of Eton and under the brown stock-brick railway
viaduct, endlessly arching its way over this flat-as-a-pancake Thames
valley country, to the blackthorn-edged road which leads to a very
dim place called Eton Wick. It is full of mid-fifties housing estates,
blossom trees and concrete lamp posts, and beyond it the road
crosses a cattle grid on to the common. This huge piece of
pastureland, sporadically speckled with sheep, cattle, joggers, kite
flyers and ponies, belongs to the lords of the manor of Dorney and its
upkeep is settled by the villagers at the manor court each year, a
satisfactory system which has been going on for centuries.

Dorney village, which lies in Buckinghamshire, on the other side of
the common, feels half feudal and half commuter-daintified. At a
curve in the road a drive through the laurel-floored woods leads you
to the heart of the place: Dorney Court and the village church. It is
heaven on earth. A perfect little pocket of timelessness among a sea
of twentieth-century progression. The M4 motorway whirrs half a
mile away, the JCBs hover over the land which is about to become
Eton's rowing lake, and the far-off fields of hay are under houses
now. But there stands the manor house, an unperturbed survivor,
across a little meadow and backed by the ravishing Tudor church
tower. It is quintessential England – built of rose-red brick and half
timbering, straggling, oversailing, and looking as though it were
growing out of the ground like the fat sculpted yew hedges which
guard it.

The glorious thing about the house is that although it epitomizes
'olde Englande' in the Stratford upon Avon sense, it is *not* over-
restored and is more like a familiar old relation than a face-lifted film

star. It has changed and adapted endlessly over the last 600 years and its waving roofs and barge-boarded gables are woven together like tapestry. It really doesn't matter where the medieval starts or the Victorian begins because it has a completely homogenous feel and demonstrates that as long as a family loves a house it will go on living and adapting on a relative shoestring. The Palmers, who have owned it since the 1500s, have never had any money to speak of; they have simply patched it up as and when it is necessary. Although the house is listed Grade I, Peregrine Palmer has never applied for, nor received, any grant money. He prefers to do things in his own time as his father did before him. He is currently mending a section of wall which completely collapsed because the original timbers had rotted. These will be replaced by seasoned oak and the roof tiles will be new hand-mades. 'They will last longer than the best second-hands,' he explains. The building firm Billinghurst has long been looking after Dorney and understands its quirks.

Inside, the layout of Dorney Court has changed little since the fifteenth century. A protective and cocooning feeling pervades the house. Each room feels like a safe haven, panelled to the hilt, and in the cosy parlour several turkey carpets laid on top of each other, and a huge open fire, serve to keep the room snug and the watery Thames dampness at bay. All around there is an eccentric mix of family treasures – from an early portrait of 'Seven Eminent Turks' brought back from Constantinople by Sir Roger Palmer, an ambassador to Charles II, to the present Palmer's lumbering Old English sheepdog and its sporty little terrier companion. The spectacular great hall with its original roof has linenfold panelling, there is a haunted bedroom which Peregrine Palmer is too frightened to sleep in, and a pink thirties bathroom suite in an oversailing bathroom where the pipes freeze up regularly. It's a *lived in* and loved house, and feels like it. Ancestors have protested against the Elizabethan style in the past – a Victorian Palmer got fed up with the low-ceilinged dining room and made himself a mock William and Mary one, and an eighteenth-century Palmer tacked on a flimsy classical front which was later taken off. There was never enough money for a radical and irreversible overhaul.

The church, cheek by jowl with the house which rambles on to almost touch it, is calm and un-Victorianized and still has a family box pew – albeit half the height it was originally. The nave and chancel were ceiled for the sake of warmth and comfort. In the little north chapel is the splendid Garrard tomb (sometimes spelt Gerrard). The Garrards were grocers who owned the court and gave their name to Gerrards Cross; the Palmers married into the family in the sixteenth century.

EDENSOR

Derbyshire

THE Peak District is a country of dark peaty moors, of waterfalls and caverns, zigzags of loose gritstone walls, and deep and dramatic valleys. 'There are things in Derbyshire,' wrote Bryon, 'as noble as Greece or Switzerland.' Give me Buxton and Chatsworth over Greece, and Castleton country over Switzerland any day. It is 'more wonderful country than you thought England had . . . where London seems a thousand miles away,' wrote Henry Thorold in his *Shell Guide to Derbyshire*.

Here, in the heart of the Chatsworth estate, huddled below New Piece Wood and encircled by a wall, lies Edensor, probably the grandest village in England. Anyone arriving by way of smaller roads winding from Rowsley or Bakewell must surely feel their hearts miss a beat as they round the corner and see Chatsworth for the first time. It is set like a fairytale palace in the gentle village of the Derwent with Edensor an elegantly suitable distance away on the other side of the road. It is a false village, in that it has not grown haphazardly, but it is visionary; it was designed an an ideal. Most of England's villages were natural evolutions, expanding or diminishing over the centuries. But Edensor was created virtually from scratch in the 1830s, when the road from Beeley to Baslow was realigned, changing the outline of the park. It gave the sixth Duke of Devonshire the opportunity to upgrade the housing of his employees and also to romanticize the atmosphere of the park. Much of the old village, which stood below the present one, was swept away, save for one house inhabited by an old man, Thomas Holmes, whom the duke did not wish to disturb.

It was the land-owning classes of the eighteenth century who first created these model villages, when the fashion for verdant landscapes around the house was all the rage and an untidy village near at hand was like a mote in the eye to any cultivated gentleman. Scores of villages were razed to the ground and new ones built outside the park gates, often with devastating political and aesthetic effect.

While model villages started out as fairly plain and practical housing estates, built in the local style, by the nineteenth century they had become wildly fanciful. The 'bachelor' duke, who never did things by halves, decided to tour some famous examples in an effort to gain inspiration. He took with him his gardener, Joseph Paxton. They visited Nuneham Courtenay in Oxfordshire, where the neat, straight rows of cottages did not impress the duke, but at Blaise Hamlet near Bristol, the Picturesque creation of the architect John Nash, he was knocked for six. 'The most perfect cottages . . . I ever saw . . . Paxton was struck with the chimneys,' he wrote in his diary.

So Edensor became a Picturesque village on a grandiose scale and boasted the most eclectic mix of styles imaginable, including Norman, Swiss, Tudor and Gothic Revival, in what the present duchess calls 'lion-coloured stone'. Paxton was in charge of the layout, his assistant John Robertson saw to the details, and the duke took a strong interest. Some of the 'cottages' are hardly bigger than a caravan, some are as large as rectories, and St Peter's is exaggeratedly spectacular, with a spire which would suit a sizeable market town. Sir George Gilbert Scott was responsible for enlarging the fourteenth-century church under the auspices of the austere and deeply religious seventh duke.

The village is a riproaring success. It has survived the test of time by being well built and carefully maintained. When James Gladstone applied to Newbury District Council to build a model village on Picturesque lines in the 1980s, he was refused. Gladstone's was a visionary scheme an appropriate site, like the duke's. When the latter returned from Europe in 1839, glad to be back, he wrote in his diary, 'Fine day. Happy village. New cottages.' Newbury will never know how happy it could have been.

ELMLEY CASTLE

Worcestershire

WORCESTERHIRE, one of England's smallest counties, is only about thirty miles wide by thirty-five miles long. People chatter about Gloucestershire or Oxfordshire, but seldom about apple-orcharded Worcestershire, that county of damson-coloured brick and black-and-white houses and cottages, secure and safe with their skirtings of fruit trees which become mists of white and pink blossom in spring. Worcestershire was always the most fertile of counties and harbours a wealth of good gardeners – one of whose creation is to be found on the way into Elmley Castle.

Elmley Castle is a glorious village. It is tucked under beautiful Bredon Hill, justly one of the most sung hills in England. If you approach it from the east, through proper plum country with laden September trees, on the very outskirts of the village you will come on Elms Cottage – spick and span and surrounded by one of those prize-winning gardens you cannot believe is real. The lawns are of a smooth green velvet and each rich and gaudy bedding plant is grown to its exemplary biggest and best.

On past Elms Cottage is the main village street, pleasurably wide, with a line of trees on one side guarding a tiny stream. Near the church, the street turns into a little village square; here is the black-and-white pub, the Queen Elizabeth, where inevitably she is supposed to have slept. Opposite, there is a narrow lane between two cottages leading out on to a wide green where cricket matches linger well on into summer Sunday evenings. Beside the green is a dull estate of brick council houses and, beside the church, an equally undistinguished sixties estate, a sort of early Brookside, full of shrub-gardened culs-de-sac, but laced with mature trees. The strange thing is that both of these newish developments have somehow settled in without any song and dance. Perhaps this is because the houses have not been packed in using every available inch; the place still has a feeling of generosity.

There is something tremendously satisfactory about Elmley Castle. 'A true midland medley of half-timber, brick, and stone,' wrote Humphrey Packington in Batsford's *English Villages and Hamlets* in the 1930s. 'One of the most peaceful and comfortable of little places. May heaven preserve you from all molestation, most loved of all Worcestershire villages!'

In the parish church of St Mary there is a model of the castle which gave the village its name. Long since gone, it was the stronghold of that ancient English family, the Beauchamps. Then came the Savages, who built a house in the 1550s, but this, with its additions, was demolished in the early 1960s. The Savages have left their mark, however, in one of the best monuments in all Worcestershire. Exquisitely sculpted in translucent alabaster lie three figures; one is a girl holding a baby in her arms, while four little Jacobean boys kneel at their feet.

To the west of the Queen Elizabeth pub a lane leads along and steeply up towards the irresistible mysteries of Bredon Hill, a leftover of the Costwold escarpment, which was picked up and thrown out into the Vale of Evesham like a giant molehill on a lush and verdant lawn. On the way up you pass half-timbered and stone cottages of great beauty; beside one is the biggest pear tree I have ever seen. The metalled road ends at a gate and becomes a stone-based track which cuts through a high-banked russet-earthed tunnel of arching nut trees with ferns beneath. Suddenly the tunnel ends and you are out on to steep, ancient, tumpy ground where sheep graze under old hawthorn trees. It is the sort of land that has looked like this for ever.

Age-old tracks cut deep into the hillside leading over to other villages which encircle Bredon's foot – Great Comberton, Bredon's Norton, Kemerton, Overbury, Ashton under Hill. With each step that you climb you see more of Worcestershire and gradually what seems like the whole of England is spread below you into the blue distance, conjured up perhaps most famously by A. E. Housman.

> In summertime on Bredon
>> The bells they sound so clear;
> Round both the shires they ring them
>> In steeples far and near,
>> A happy sound to hear.
>
> Here of a Sunday morning
>> My love and I would lie,
> And see the coloured counties,
>> And hear the larks so high
>> About us in the sky.

When William Cobbett, who foretold the wrecking of England, rode up Bredon Hill, he described its surroundings as being 'one of the very richest spots in England. These rivers, particularly the Severn, go through, and sometimes overflow, the finest meadows of which it is possible to form an idea.' Though the motorway whines beside the village of Bredon and industry spills out into the countryside, I think he would still find that looking across his beloved England from these heights would lift his heart.

THE ISLE OF ELY

Cambridgeshire

Y OU can catch a small stopping turbo train from Platform 10a at King's Cross Station in London and travel through suburbs and dated new towns and quiet halts, all the way to Ely. Past Arsenal's great football ground at Highbury, through Welwyn and Hitchin and on into the heart of silvery Hertfordshire where the brick turns paler and the chalk downs roll around Royston. At Cambridge there is a quiet little station of buff brick in restrained late Regency style and as you pull out you might catch a brief glimpse of glorious King's College Chapel and St John's tower, and you might see a team of under-graduate rowers skimming along in an eight as the train crosses the wide river Cam.

At the village of Waterbeach a different country altogether begins – the strange chessboard of unfamiliar Fens. Beside the tiny halt, where no one gets on or off the train, there is an old orchard with bee hives beneath the apple trees. The line is raised up above its floodable surroundings, waterless now, though Waterbeach was once described as a 'small fen archipelago'. The village's most famous son was Charles Spurgeon, who laid the foundation stone for a little brick Baptist chapel. He became one of the most famous preachers in England, drawing enormous crowds and baptizing followers by the dozen in the Cam. A little to the north is a lovely group of buildings comprising Denny Abbey, which is set on what was once a tiny island, in the archipelago. Much of the extensive abbey remains have become part of a farm's steddings, converted over the centuries since the abbey's demise and now looked after by English Heritage. You can see it across the wide North Fen as the train trundles on towards Ely.

Over Stretham Mere, on either side of the track, the fields of spinach stretch. Then cabbages, then huge empty plots of bitter-chocolate-coloured earth. There are lines of poplars every so often to break the biting wind which blows in relentlessly from the North Sea. Lonely, plain little houses stick up abruptly now and then, as do red-roofed villages whose cottages huddle together among trees. Past Little Thetford you begin to see the wondrous cathedral of Ely. If you were sitting with the driver of the train, or if you were travelling from anywhere else, you would have seen it many miles before. But even if you have approached it a hundred times before, its scale never ceases to astonish, and the mere fact that it was built from the beginning of the eleventh century by human hand alone, to the glory of God and not commerce, never ceases to move. In the early morning, when there is a mist on the Fens, the cathedral rises like a gigantic ship on a pale sea and is probably as thrilling a sight as England can afford.

Ely Station is Cambridge's architectural twin, with its iron columns and fancy spandrels supporting its roof, but on Platform 1 it offers a second-hand paperback bookstall. You can easily walk up the long slow hill from the station to the cathedral – it takes about ten minutes unless you get waylaid at the Tuck Shop, which you pass beside a small tree-strewn green where boys from King's School linger. The steepness of Ely's hill is surprising in this pancake countryside, but explains why such a great cathedral was built here, for it was one of the largest islands in this once water-covered landscape.

St Ethelreda's monastery on the 'island of eels', of which she became abbess over 1,300 years ago, suffered under the Danes. (Ethelreda's popular name was St Audrey, and the Pilgrims' Fair which took place at Ely was soon called St Awdrey's Fair. The word 'tawdry' became part of the English language after hucksters sold cheap silk neckcloths at the fair and called them 'St Awdrey's chains' or, more commonly, 'tawdries'.) The monastery was refounded in the tenth century and under the first Norman abbot the building of the cathedral began. It would take an entire book to sing its praises adequately.

The length and height of it are awe-inspiring, and the sheer bravery of building it dumb-founding. Imagine the windy night of 22 February 1322: the monks were retiring to their cells when the great Norman tower fell into the choir and the earth shook all around. Alan of Walsingham then replaced it with the Octogan tower – the most graceful feat of Gothic engineering imaginable. If you sit under it you can look up at the eight arches, four opening to the arms of the cathedral and four to the clerestory. Off the north transept, a doorway leads to the supremely graceful Lady Chapel, built of the palest stone, like icing, and with huge clear-glass windows.

The small town of Ely clusters around the cathedral. The bishop's palace and handsome houses surround the 'college' or close. King's School is housed in breathtaking medieval buildings with Norman undercrofts beside the thistled parkland dipping down towards the fenland, and fine monastic buildings stretch along one side of the High Street.

FARMCOTE

Gloucestershire

THERE are those who would feel nervous about coming to Farmcote: the sort who describe driving conditions as 'shocking' in Devon and Cornwall because of the single-track roads and high banks. (When I have fallen asleep on the train going home and been carried to a station beyond mine, the taxi drivers who bring me back at midnight inevitably say, 'I'm glad I don't have to drive along this road every day of the week, it's positively dangerous,' as they wind along a perfectly ordinary narrow road towards our village.)

'Sticking to minor roads. . .' wrote John Wells and Brian Rees for a musical called *The Birds*. We sing it in the car:

> . . . and leaving our cares behind us
> Where nobody hopes to find us,
> > we go.
> Happily making tracks
> and turning our backs
> on things we know. . .

Farmcote is in what some would call 'the back of beyond'. The minor road dips down from Lynes Barn Farm towards the dead-end hamlet of Farmcote. It trails along a narrow lane which peters out and becomes a track, running through old countryside, too steep in places to plough, and in July the sheep-cropped grassland is covered in lady's slipper. The banks brim with meadow crane's-bill, hogweed, yarrow, lady's bedstraw, scabious, knapweed and sudden patches of rosebay willowherb. I have heard that there are greater butterfly orchids, green hellebores and herb Paris in secret places in the surrounding area, and that you used to be able to find the Pasque flower, bee and fly orchids and the rare red hellebore, but these are all now gone.

If you have not come on the road you can walk up from the ruins of Hailes Abbey, which lie in the valley below. Hailes was founded by Richard, Earl of Cornwall, the brother of Henry II, to fulfil a vow he had made after escaping from a shipwreck off the Isles of Scilly in 1252. His son then presented the abbey with the 'Blood of Hailes', which was authenticated by Pope Urban IV as being the real Redeemer's Blood. As a result, Hailes became a great centre for pilgrimage and the ancient, partly cobbled track which leads up into Cotswold Hills was a much-used pilgrims' way. It climbs steeply, hanging between a fruit farm and well-shot laurel-speckled woods until it reaches the heights of Farmcote, set on the eastern slopes of a wide, wild valley.

'The scene is positively startling', wrote Herbert Evans in his *Highways and Byways in Oxfordshire and the Costwolds* at the turn of the century. It still is. The middle distance is filled with Worcestershire – beautiful Bredon hill, with Dumbleton Hill before it like a beached whale. Beyond, in the blue distance, are the Malvern Hills and, beyond them, Herefordshire and the Welsh Marches.

It's a fine view indeed from Farmcote, whose original name was Ferncote – derived from Fern and Cott, meaning wood. The hamlet has been connected to Guiting Power throughout its long history and is now no more than a handful of Cotswold stone buildings. The star of these is a small Saxon chapel of ease dedicated to St Faith. It is a haven of utter peace: golden without and whitewashed within. The roof is barn-like, with timbers a thousand years old. At the east end there is a wonky Saxon stone arch, which once led through to a lost apse and is now blocked off. The sixteenth- and seventeenth-century furnishings of pews, communion rail, pulpit and clerk's desk really are quite beautiful – calm, settled and well worn, they afford an extraordinary atmosphere of tranquillity. There is a simple Norman font, and tucked into the corner of this tiny place is a graceful Elizabethan monument whose pedimented canopy holds up columns of pale gold stone to shelter the stiff, recumbent and beruffed figures of John Stratford and his wife Ann Walwyn.

Their presence is strong, and on coming out into the small churchyard you can glimpse beyond some trees their house, Great Farmcote. A fine seventeenth-century porch clings to the small, ancient part of the house, but the majority of what is now a farmhouse is a Victorian Gothic addition. Below, and hanging over the edge of the valley, is a good barn and range of farm buildings, once tiled and now roofed with asbestos and corrugated iron. The Stratford family owned the manor of Farmcote from the fourteenth century onwards, producing an archbishop of Canterbury, a bishop of London and a bishop of Chichester from among their ranks, who would all have known this hillside and this holy place very much as it is today.

FORD AND FLODDEN

Northumberland

Beyond Wooler, 'Gateway to the Cheviots' (pronounced Cheeviots by the Scots), between their high hills and the North Sea the road leads through a wide valley towards Scotland. There, on an upward sweep, Ford Castle stands out like a toy fort, with its model village nestling behind. As you apporach, you see that this is no rough and abandoned border fortress, but kempt and cosily Victorianized, thanks to the beautiful young widow Louisa, Countess of Waterford. In 1859 she retired here from Curraghmore, the Waterford's premier home in Ireland, on the death of her glamorous and much-loved husband Henry, a brilliant horseman who was killed out hunting at the age of forty. Lousia turned the castle into her home and made the estate village into her idea of Utopia. She rebuilt many of the cottages and formalized the street. The doorway of the village smithy is in the form of a giant stone horseshoe, but it is the village school which is the star of the show. Here Lousia, who was a proficient artist, painted a series of religious murals using the villagers as her models. The school closed down in 1957 but has since served as the village hall, alive with concerts, over-sixties get-togethers, bowling competitions and country dancing. The Lady Waterford Hall now houses more of her watercolours, many of them of dead and dying children which echo her sadness at having none. It is a rewarding place to visit, well cared for by the neighbouring curator Pat Hodgson, whose cat 'Lenin' stalks the hall.

Ford Castle is now rented by the Northumberland Education Authority which, apart from filling it with fifties office furniture, has not touched the snug and panelled splendour of Lousia's decoration. The comfortable impression it now gives belies its violent past. For over 2,500 years this fiercely feudal border country was a battleground between the ever-warring people of England and Scotland. It was here at Ford that James IV of Scotland had his headquarters before the fateful Battle of Flodden. Here, in the fields below, he crossed the alder-edged river Till, a tributary of the great Tweed, on the way to his sad demise.

> Tweed says to Til'
> 'What gars ye rin sae still?'
> Says Til' to Tweed,
> 'Though ye run wi' speed,
> And I rin slaw,
> Whaur ye droon ar man,
> I droon twa.'

Flodden Field lies a few miles away beside the small village of Branxton. The stark memorial, erected in 1910 'to the brave of both nations' on a rise above the great wide landscape, is as gloomy as the atmosphere that hangs over the field. Here, on 9 September 1513, James IV was killed along with nine or ten thousand of his fellow Scotsmen. His body was wrapped in what remained of the royal standard and laid in the little church of St Paul's, Branxton. Later he was buried in an unmarked grave at St Michael's, Cornhill, in London. He had been on his way to help his old allies the French and his army was using some new-fangled unfamiliar French weapons. Although they were on higher ground than the English, they took the decision to come down Branxton Hill; as they descended the ground became unexpectedly boggy and in a period of just two hours a proud army had ceased to exist. The English lost only a thousand or two; the Scots had not only lost their king but also the chiefs of nearly all their clans. Flodden was the last medieval battle to be fought on English soil. Never again were knights to fight in armour, their personal standards flying. Never again were arrows, swords and spears to be the decisive weapons.

It is hard to walk about here without thinking of the many unkown soldiers lying beneath your feet, but one of the most uplifting and unexpected glories of this border country is John Farnington's garden in Branxton, hard by. Behind his modest semi-detached pebbledashed villa is one of the most inventive small gardens in England. It is filled to the brim with life-sized concrete sculptures of every animal under the sun and every local hero. All are painted in life-like colours and narrow winding paths weave among them. Every few yards a motto or life maxim confronts the eye: 'Each days is a little life, through combat to victory.' There is a replica of the Monarch of the Glen, of Bob Fraser, a famous border shepherd, of a jaunty lady riding to hounds in amongst a menagerie of rhinoceroses, kangaroos, flamingos and pigs. No one must miss this garden: it is a veritable work of art. John Farrington died in 1990 and his daughter now looks after it. Entry is free but donations are welcome to help with the upkeep. In fact, the garden deserves a grant.

FOTHERINGHAY

Northamptonshire

FROM wherever you approach Fotheringhay, you cannot fail to be startled by the grandeur of its church, St Mary and All Saints, which stands on a slight rise above a small and unassuming limestone village. You will probably come along small roads from Warmington or Oundle, Nassington or Woodnewton, but much the best way to get there is by boat. The river Nene snakes though the surrounding meadows on its languorous way through the rigid fens towards the Wash. Last year a couple who had travelled by boat from Surrey moored at Fotheringhay. They came down the Thames to the Grand Union Canal and up to Northampton, down the Ouse to Downham Market, then upstream through the fens on the river Nene to Fotheringhay.

East of the church and closer still to the river is an uneven, sheep-grazed mound beside the farm – the sort of romantic brambled, hawthorned place which you might imagine to be the vestiges of a lost village. It is in fact that remains of a large Norman castle with inner and outer courts and inner and outer moats, which commanded the ancient river crossing and surrounding district. Its destruction by James I (and VI of Scotland) was total. He wished to obliterate all evidence of its exixtence, so ashamed was he of what had taken place there.

Fotheringhay (pronounced with a silent 'g') is where Mary Queen of Scots 'passed out of th'entire into the hall within the said castle of Ffotheringhaie . . . with an apauled countenance stept up to the scaffold in the said hall and then and there made for her death'. Mary had been moved here from Charleby in Staffordshire on 25 September 1586. Her trial took place on 14 and 15 October and she was pronounced guilty of treason on 25 October. Queen Elizabeth signed the warrant for her execution on 1 February 1587. She was executed a week later.

If you stand on the grassy tump and look out over the quiet, undulating pastureland it is hard to imagine the macabre incidents which took place here 400 years ago. According to eye witnesses, when Mary was lead to the block she was 'apparelled in a kinde of joye'. But the executioner did not have an easy time. When her head was eventually severed he tried to lift it up by the hair to show it to the spectators, but because her hair was a wig the head rolled away from him under the scaffold. Her dog, which had been hiding beneath her skirts, refused to leave and lay 'between her head and shoulders'. Queen Elizabeth can hardly have slept easily for the rest of her life.

Fotheringhay had seen happier and more constructive royal times, if no less macabre. Edmund de Langley, the son of Edward III, planned a college here, but it was his son, the 'fatte' Duke of York who actually founded it in the early fifteenth century. A few years later he was 'smouldered to death' at the Battle of Agincourt. His body was then boiled and brought back to Fotheringhay for burial. Richard III, our most engimatic king, was born and spent the first six years of his life here.

The church used to be twice the size it is now. What you see is all that is left of a large collegiate church – like those which are still intact at Warwick, Crediton or Arundel. As a result, the size and splendour of its great octagonal lantern look faintly out of proportion with the shortened nave, whose huge Perpendicular windows and elegant flying-buttressed clerestory belong to something much grander than an ordinary parish church. Inside, it is fan-vaulted and has a beautiful font and pulpit. In the field between the church and river the remains of the college are still tantalizingly visible and in the village you can see what is left of two medieval inns, the New Inn, now a house, and the Old Inn, a row of cottages.

Northamptonshire conjures up no definable image in the public mind and yet, as Juliet Smith points out in her *Shell Guide*, 'this county with its great churches, houses, its placid landscapes and its stone villages, deserves to be far more widely known'. Long may Fotheringhay remain the rural backwater that it is. Long may the new type of 'facility'-demanding visitor remain ignorant of the uneventful beauty of the county of 'spires, squires and mires'. As long as no signposts point in tourist code to Fotheringhay, no toilet and nappy-changing facilities, or gift shops, or audio-visual interpretation centres are advertised, the crowds may not want to come. The castle mound is owned neither by the National Trust nor English Heritage but by the local farming family of Gould, who prohibit entry between Christmas and New Year merely in order to establish their rights; the rest of the time they let cattle, sheep, or you and I roam over it.

FRAMPTON ON SEVERN

Gloucestershire

FRAMPTON ON SEVERN is one of the most beautiful villages in England. This is a little-known fact, perhaps because it lies in a strange and forgotten area, stranded between the M5 motorway and the mile-wide river Severn. It is flat, watery vale country with views westwards across the river to the Forest of Dean and the mountains of Wales in the blue distance beyond. To the east, the sudden Cotswold escarpment rises from the flatness like a theatre backdrop. The skies are forever Peter Scott-ish, for Frampton lies just north of Slimbridge, his bird sanctuary, and hundreds of ducks and geese still fly homeward across the sunset and the dawn, just as he depicted.

One of the reasons why Frampton remains unwrecked is because most of the village is tucked away in a cul-de-sac. A small road threads its way through the middle of a great wide village green, almost three quarters of a mile long. There may be other huge village greens but I know none more lovely, nor more lordly. A manor house, a half-timbered barn, a court, a brick farmhouse with a large duck pond before it, groups of small houses and thatched cottages spread themselves generously along its edges.

It is called Rosmund's Green, after 'Fair Rosamund' Clifford, who was born at the ancient, rambling, half-timbered Manor Farm on the west side of the green. Rosamund's Bower, a projecting first-floor window which looks out towards passers-by, is said to be where Henry II first saw her as he rode by. He fell instantly in love with her and she became his openly acknowledged mistress; her untimely death in 1176 was shrouded in mystery.

One legend has it that Queen Eleanor led her to the middle of a maze by leaving a silken thread for her to follow and then poisoned her; another that she was murdered near Woodstock – bled to death in a hot bath. The pink-and-white striped *Rosamunda* rose is called after her.

Descendants of the Clifford family still live at Manor Farm and still use a nearby fifteenth-century barn of silvery weathered-wood squares with wattle and daub between, in which to store wool. Across the green from the farm, half hidden by chestnut trees, ilexes and a long wall, is Frampton Court, also owned by the Cliffords. It was built in the 1730s of bright golden limestone and is startlingly beautiful. An elegant sweep of steps rises to the front door at the centre of the main block, and there are small wings on either side with daringly high chimneys. Inside is some of the best woodwork in England – the pannelling, doorways, cupboards, cornices and balusters are exquisitely worked and there is an eighteenth-century dog gate at the bottom of the stairs, which concertinas out from the wall with perfect precision in a series of curly crisscrosses.

If you look out over the park with its sheets of water you can imagine the five Clifford daughters who lived here in the nineteenth century and never married. They catalogued the flora of the area with exquisite watercolours and descriptions which were discovered in the attic here at the Court a decade ago and made into a book called *Frampton Flora*. In the garden, and visible from the green, there is a Strawberry Hill Gothic garden house at the end of a rectangular canal in which it is reflected.

Beyond the green's end the road bends and becomes an ordinary village street until, as the houses begin to peter out, it stops at the beautiful church of St Mary, set alone and apart. A Judas tree hangs over the churchyard wall, and you can see a gravestone carved with a weeping willow by John Pearce. The church windows are mostly of clear glass and it feels airy and light as you enter. A track continues on to Splatt Bridge, which spans the Gloucester-to-Sharpness canal and swings open to let the barges through. Beside it is the canal-keeper's cottage, like a little Doric temple with a pediment and fluted columns in perfect Cheltenham-style Regency. Then there is marsh, merging with the muddy creeks and inlets of a swooping bend in the river Severn called The Noose. When I last went a thick mist hung everywhere and I was happy to turn back towards the village I knew.

GODMANCHESTER

Huntingdonshire

How many people do you know who have been to Godmanchester? How many people even know where it is? John Major might, because across a fourteenth-century stone bridge lies his home at Huntingdon. But on the whole it is little known, unsung, and one of the grandest little towns in England. When the Godmanchester fire engine turned up to help extinguish the fires in London during the Blitz, no one had ever heard of the place.

'Once a noble city, and now a pleasant town,' noted the monkish Henry of Huntingdon in the twelfth century. For during the Roman occupation of Britain it had been an extraordinarily important place. Godmanchester controlled the crossing of Ermine Street over the great river Ouse and was a stopping-off place for soldiers on their way north. In consequence the area is rich in Roman remains of inns, temples, baths and markets. Archaeologists will certainly have heard of Godmanchester and their hearts may flutter with excitement at the mere mention of the name.

As a child I was taught to pronounce it 'Gumster' (just as I was taught to say 'Weston-Super-Marry' for Weston-Super-Mare, 'New Burg' for Newbury and 'Brickleton' for Brightwalton). As I grew up and the light dawned that my parents had made me a laughing stock of the geography class I dropped these fancy ways. However, when reading about Godmanchester recently I discovered that it had indeed been called Gumecestre in Roman times; my dad's passionate love of Latin had proved him right as usual.

The Ouse dominates the town – that glorious river down which you can boat from King's Lynn to Bedford: 'The most agreeable circumstance in this part of the world', thought the local poet William Cowper, who wrote of it often:

The poplars are fell'd, farewell to the shade
And the whispering sound of the cool colonnade,
The winds play no longer, and sing in the leaves,
Nor Ouse on his bosom their image receives.

As it passes through Godmanchester, the river's swan- and duck-strewn bosom receives images of the most elegant of bridges, epitomized by a slow-arched Chinese one from which the river seems to spread in every direction as it forms inlets here and there like great fingers across the flat, willowy meadowlands. If you stand on this bridge you can get the feel of the town very well – it is still, more or less, in the same polygonal shape of Roman times – with St Mary's Church rising high above the jumble of disparate red-tiled rooflines and the gardens sloping down to the water's edge. Follow the river upstream, by way of two smaller bridges and waterfalls, and from the Lock Bridge you will get the best view of Portholme Meadow, said to be the largest water meadow in England (226 acres). Often flooded in winter, nearly always good for a spectacular sunset, it has been common land for centuries and grazed by cattle from the many farms in and around the town. In the distance lies Hinchingbrooke, where Samuel Pepys often stayed with his cousins. He described walking with his father in Portholme Meadow in October 1662 and watching 'the country-maids milking their cows there . . . and to see with what mirth they all came home together in pomp with their milk, and sometimes they have musique to go before them.'

Apart from the Ouse and the meadow, the most striking feature of Godmanchester is the quality of its domestic architecture. There are substantial seventeenth-century timber-framed houses standing on the pavement. The Gables is one of the finest and was a farm until quite recently. If you knock on the door the owner, Dr Charles Looker, whose family came to the town in 1805, may let you look at the huge barn behind, and the dovecote with its 3,000 pigeon holes.

But the eighteenth-century houses stand out most. On Post Street, with its garden backing on to the river, stands Island Hall, built in

1730, proud, prosperous and completely satisfactory. Then there is The Holme, built of red-and-yellow brick. On West Street there is the beautiful mid-Georgian Farm Hall, a perfect red-brick doll's house, commanding a good view across the street to its own lime avenue and little canal which lead the eye on to the infinite pastures of Portholme Meadow. William Cobbett did tend to eulogize, but few would not feel wonder at seeing what he described in 1822 as 'by far the most beautiful meadows that I ever saw in my life'.

HELMINGHAM

Suffolk

SOME of the Suffolk countryside has been wrecked. Between villages like Cotton, Gipping and Middlewood Green there are hedgeless prairies of spray-scorched cereals stretching to the near horizons under huge skies. Stranded farmhouses (there are five or six hundred moated farmsteads in Suffolk) appear as mere dots in the landscape, and you wonder if you are perhaps in the Fens by mistake. If you are travelling in the open air you will notice that the wind is particularly relentless and the cold extraordinary, even on a mild spring day. When you reach the protection of a hedge or a wood you feel a wave of warmth; it is like walking into a centrally heated room from outside. You *long* for the hedges. I talked to a horse-dealer from a farm near Mickfield who drives his wife in a pony and cart to do the shopping in Debenham every Thursday. For fifty years he has done this, but since they took the hedges away the couple have needed to wear over coats in summer.

Travelling on eastwards, a tract of true Suffolk begins and as you approach Helmingham your spirits soar. Here is an oasis of loveliness, and a park and a half to boot. It consists of 400 acres of ancient oak trees, some of which are up to 900 years old. They lean this way and that, each one more majestic than the last with their immense girths and occasional stag branches. John Constable, whose brother was steward at Helmingham, lived for some time in the rectory and painted a number of versions of *A Dell in Helmingham Park* (the oak he depicted is still here). Two large herds of red and fallow deer which have been here for centuries roam the park, as well as Highland cattle and Soay sheep. Towards Pettaugh a high brick obelisk pierces the sky above the oaks, built in 1860 from the bricks of a collapsed walled garden. It stands on The Mound (hills in

Suffolk are few and far between), which was used by Helmingham volunteers to practise their musketry during the Napoleonic Wars. At the western edge of the park stands the silvery flint church of St Mary with its sixteenth-century tower.

A relatively young avenue of oaks planted in 1700 leads up to Helmingham Hall, this rose-red beauty of a house. The stronghold of the Tollemache family, who have lived in Suffolk since the eleventh century, it is surrounded by a wide and defensive moat; the two drawbridges are drawn up every night. The Hall, basically half timbered and built in Henry VIII's time, has been enhanced over the generations – aggrandized by the Tudor Tollemaches, brick faced by the Georgian Tollemaches, castellated by the Regency Tollemaches and adorned with diamond-pattern bricks by the early Victorian Tollemaches. The shape of the house, with its internal cobbled courtyard, has never changed.

If previous generations of Tollemaches have proudly maintained and enhanced the house – with occasional lapses – the present generation love the place no less. The house glows with the pride of being well cared for, but it is the garden which is their gift to the place. It is almost too good to be true – the sort of garden few of us could achieve even with a wealth of gardeners. It is inspired. On the west side of the house there is a large walled garden which is surrounded by its own deep moat, on the sloping banks of which are a profusion of wild flowers, from orchids, cowslips and fritilleries in the spring to corn cockle, moon daisies and columbines in the summer. The lawn in front of the entrance is approached across a grass causeway, and set with a formal box-edged rose and bedding-out garden.

Once inside the wrought-iron gates of the walled garden, your eye is led straight to the brick piers at the far end by long lengths of herbaceous border spilling, by late summer, over a grass path whose perfect edges are like freshly cut cake. The garden is divided into eight large vegetable plots, just as it has been since Elizabethan times. There is a series of iron arches which each year form tunnels of sweet peas, runner beans and ornamental gourds. Beyond the safe, enclosing comfort of the walls and out across the moat on another grass causeway you reach the wild flowered orchard and tennis court and return to the house down either the north or south spring-flowered grass walks outside the walled garden.

On the east side of the house is a rose garden containing myriad old species mixed with lavender and foxgloves, almost enclosed in a yew room, with a backdrop of the house on one side and the oaks of the park on the other. Before it is a box parterre echoing the brickwork diamonds on the house and incorporating the present Tollemache's initials.

HELMSLEY AND BRANSDALE

Yorkshire

VENTURE up Bransdale and you will find unadulterated Yorkshire: first through a strung-out little village called Carlton, whose yellow-stone cottages with red pantiled roofs have low walled gardens and straight flower-lined paths to their front doors; then down over Bogmire Gill and up past a strange, dour chapel sitting among Scots pines and reeking of episcopalianism; on past oaks and strange mounds until the long, purple-heather horizon of Pockley Moor is before you. Eventually, when the heather becomes bracken and a slow descent takes you past some gloomy fir plantations, the emerald oasis of Bransdale appears in the valley below, crisscrossed with walls and hedges and sprinkled with farmhouses set among their steddings and trees. Places called Toad Hole, Smout House, Spout House, Cowl House, Cow Syke, Stork House and Bog House cling to the winding lanes in this, the remote head of the dale, surrounded by high, looming moors and cut off from the world in winter. 'Mountains I have no love for; they are accidents of nature thrown up in volcanic agony,' wrote Herbert Read the art historian, who was brought up on a neighbouring farm in Ryedale. 'But moors and fells are moulded by gentle forces, by rainwater and wind, and are human in their contours and proportions, inducing affection rather than awe.' At the dale's end there is a Victorian shooting lodge in the classical style and a chapel. You can return on the other side of the valley, and there could be nowhere better to come home to than Helmsley.

You pronounce it 'Hemmsley' – this star of a market town set on an eminence, gently sloping towards the banks of the Rye. The source of the Rye is right at the upper end of Bilsdale; the river then passes the most romantic ruins in England – those of Rievaulx Abbey

– winds on past the grounds of Duncombe Park, skirts the town of Helmsley and then pursues a meandering course of sixteen miles through a rich and fertile vale until it falls into the Derwent a little above Malton. High above hanging woods and the ruined abbey is the long and languorous grassy stretch of Rievaulx Terrace – eighteenth-century landscape gardening at its best – with a Doric temple at one end and an Ionic at the other. It was created by Thomas Duncombe III as a place to visit for picnics from his neighbouring and rather dull early Georgian house, Duncombe Park.

Helmsley, on whose southern outskirts are the gates to Duncombe Park, is as old as the hills. The ruins of its Norman castle stand on a series of spectacular grass-covered ramparts and its market, which takes place on Fridays, is almost as old. Set in the generous square where a statue of an ermine-clad Lord Feversham (the Duncombes became the Earls of Feversham) stands under a pinnacled canopy. The great Yorkshireman Harry J. Scott, founder and editor of 'The Dalesman', wrote in the 1940s of the 'hearty goodwill in northern markets where . . . the stall holders are part of a great army of nomads, moving from market to market every day of the week with their fents and their jewellery, their fish and their vegetables and their literary fare bearing titles like *Her Last Chance, He Loved Too Well* and *Poppy's Romance* and always the stall with the freize of trousers hanging round its edge.' Today the fish stall displays fresh catches from Whitby and if the literature palls there is a good antiquarian bookshop called Rievaulx Books.

Helmsley's main trade is now tourism; it was once agriculture and linen. The atmosphere has suffered not a whit, neither have local shoppers forsaken it for Scarborough. Helmsley still has proper shops. One of my favourites is Claridges, a stationer and bookseller between the church and the main square. Mr Claridge (whose father was a Londoner, his mother a Yorkshire woman) started the shop thirty years ago. If you want good maps and guidebooks, sketch books and kind friendly ladies seeing to your needs, there is nowhere better. Sadly, Job Clarke, one of the last drapers and gentlemen's and ladies' outfitters, ended its days and emptied its windows in 1993, but the shop has now been taken over by the family firm of W. P. Brown of York, so the chainstores are still being held at bay. Mr Nicholson is another tradesman of high repute whose firm of butchers (to which he later added a grocer and off-licence) was started by his father in the thirties. It was the first firm in the North of England to be made a member of the exclusive 'Q' Guild of master butchers. Until last year Mr Nicholson hunted regularly with the neighbouring Sinnington, Middleton and Derwent packs and, less often, with the Bilsdale, the oldest hunt in Britain. 'The hill descents are a bit nerve-wracking on a thoroughbred – you need a good strong cob for that country,' he explained. Mr Nicholson became chairman of the local parish council because, he said, 'I wanted to keep Helmsley like it is.'

North-West Herefordshire

HERE is a corner of England which is paradise. It is as a lot of England should be, and isn't. Everything is on the right scale. It is a deep, steep countryside of sheep-grazed tumps and sudden, strangely shaped hills, some wooded, some sparsely scattered with trees and bushes. Between the valleys and vales, small fields are hawthorn hedged and the birdsong is deafening. There are tall, thin houses, turreted churches, uneventful chestnut-shaded villages, lots of apple orchards and occasional fields thick with buttercups. The stone varies from village to village, sometimes steel grey, sometimes dark rose, and there are black-and-white thatched cottages among the stone.

This north-west corner of Herefordshire is an area of mixed farming, with perhaps more cattle than anything else, and the farms are fairly small scale. I know that, given these conditions, it is easier to maintain a paradisial landscape, but this sort of perfection is rare, avoiding as it does the tweeness of the equivalent farming country in parts of Devon, for instance, where the cream tea and B & B signs dangle from every cob and thatch farmhouse wall the edges of villages have sprouted far-worse-than-usual dream retirement homes because of far-worse-than-usual planning authorities. There is no soft-edged cosiness here in high Herefordshire. It is unsung, unselfconscious and utterly beautiful.

When the terrain dictated the farming of England everything looked well. Since the government has been dictating it much of the countryside has been wrecked. Lately, in these green nineties, there have been efforts by an embarrassed civil service to make amends for the wrongs inflicted on the land. Galaxies of goody-goody hedge-field, wood and wildlife 'officers' and 'experts' with beatific smiles have been offering grants to amazed farmers, some of whom have neither been interested nor had time to fill in the necessary forms.

Much of the pattern of the English landscape used to be like Herefordshire – the Pewsey Vale enjoyed the same sort of mixed farming on rich pastureland where apple orchards and hedges abounded; now bits of it look like Canada's middle west. Some of the surrounding downland with its fine old turf – only ever good for sheep – was ploughed up to grow subsidized wheat. The underlying flints were sliced into millions of razor blades by powerful ploughs, so that the land could never be the same again. Farming was turned upside down.

This piece of country escaped the massacre. Its beauty, though, is not wholly down to its small farms and its patchwork-quilt fields. It has a high rainfall and, as a result, the best oak trees in the kingdom. They are everywhere: oaks growing from the hedgerows, oaks clinging to the hillsides and oaks scattered in amongst the fields at graceful intervals as though Humphry Repton had been called in to landscape the place at the end of the eighteenth century.

It is hardly surprising that two great pundits of the Picturesque movement – Uvedale Price and Richard Payne Knight – were Herefordshire squires. They abhorred Capability Brown's manicured landscapes and admired instead 'nature's negligent disguise' and the 'splendid confusion and irregularity' of Gothic architecture. Their influences are evident in the countryside around, but perhaps more than anywhere in the park of Croft Castle.

Knight was a first cousin of Elizabeth Johnes who lived at Croft. He and Price were close friends of her son Thomas. There is an avenue of seventeenth-century Spanish chestnuts planted in the park; some of the oaks over 27 feet in girth. 'In respect of these Titans and towers of time,' wrote H. J. Massingham in *The Southern Marches*, 'the final honours must go to the Parklands of Croft Castle . . .'

The girths may be an inch wider at Croft, but my final honours for the most beautiful park in the world go to Brampton Bryan, where Spanish chestnuts with diagonally twisted bark and gigantic oaks –

the vestiges of a medieval deer park – feel as old as the steep, wide bowl of hills which protect them, and the yew hedge surrounding the village church is as sumptuous and satisfactory a sight as you could wish for.

Daunts, in London's Marylebone High Street, the best shop in the country for modern English topography, has enough books on the Cotswolds, the West Country, East Anglia, the Yorkshire Dales and the Lakes to fill several lorries, but you could easily carry the section on Shropshire and Herefordshire in a bicycle basket. It is too far away from motorways and fast trains to bring more than a light sprinkling of visitors.

HEYDON

Norfolk

HEYDON is little known, on the way to nowhere, quiet, unadulterated and as near to the pastoral idyll as anywhere in England.

As in so many other counties, huge tracts of Norfolk's countryside were devastated in the fifties, sixties and early seventies by agribusiness. Fields the length of a furlong – as far as a horse could pull the plough without a breather – went out of the window.

Today regimented rows of hawthorn whips in plastic wraps or chicken-wire are planted to re-clothe the desert. This looks hopeful, but too tidy. You cannot recreated overnight the idiosyncratic corners which nature and good husbandry create over centuries, where:

> Unkempt about those hedges blows
> An English unofficial rose!

The family who farm the Heydon land have hung on to their hedges. They didn't reap as much money as their neighbours twenty years ago, but now are the envy of all. Heydon shines, anchored by trees and woods and secret dells and well-cared-for hedges.

A wood and a park away from the main Norwich-to-Holt road, you turn off past Dog Corner and thickly bluebelled Newhall Wood to the dead-end turning for the village. Just before it, there is a glimpse of the glorious gabled Grange, lying low down an old chestnut avenue.

Brick-pedimented estate cottages, the former school, a working smithy run by the blacksmith, Jack Barber, straggle along the wide street which leads to just about the best village green you could wish for with a Gothic Revival pump in its midst. On the south side of the green is a perfect Mrs Mitford residence, cosy village Georgian covered in rose-clad trellis. The lane passes by leading towards high trees and a hidden rectory. On the north side a row of tiny gabled cottages is dwarfed by the great flint Perpendicular church behind it.

Inside, the arch over the west door is as lofty and lovely as could be, and if you look ahead to the top of the fourteenth-century rood screen you will see a white barn owl. Still and stuffed, it is meant to scare bats away. That's what the church warden told me, but I thought bats were blind. The tub-shaped font is fourteenth century and there are lots of Bulwer hatchments, monuments and a mortuary chapel.

On the fourth side of the green between the cottages there is a bow-fronted village store cum post office, run by Mr and Mrs Sutton, where you can buy fresh food and get your hair done; together with their son they run a ladies and gents hairdresser's. Just along from here is the Earle Arms, which takes its name from Erasmus Earle, the Cromwellian lawyer who bought Heydon Hall in 1650.

The village is pretty near perfect, but it is *not* quaint, nor has it an air of forced prettiness about it, like some villages. Heydon is a *working* village which manages to retain the ideal degree of unkempt beauty.

Beyond the green, through the gates, a drive leads across a sylvan park complete with Stubbs-like images of fine shiny horses grazing under oak trees to a dead-on view of Heydon Hall, a rose-red beauty of an Elizabethan house, framed by a wide flank of oak and beech behind yew hedges.

Heydon Hall faces out towards a distant chestnut avenue, ending in a view of Cawston's great church spire. It was built, with its three pinnacled gables and clustered chimneys soaring above, in the 1580s by Henry Dynne, the auditor of the exchequer, and ended up with the Bulwer family when it passed to Mrs Bulwer, Erasmus Earle's sister.

Around the house and clinging to its east side is a veritable village of mellow-brick buildings – stables, barns, clock tower, a walled *potager.* There are orchards and a garden of wide lawns and cedars. There are secret paths winding away through rhododendrons and mop-head may trees, statues, and glimpses of park and ancient sweet chestnuts with swirling, spiralling bark beyond.

HINDON

Wiltshire

THERE is an area deep in the West Country, well beyond the stark uplands of Salisbury Plain and the sheep-cropped turf around Stonehenge, where the hills are bold and rolling and set with huge woods. It is known as 'general' country because so many army officers have retired here – some because they like to hear the faint rumblings of manoeuvres on the plain, some because they have part-time jobs in Strategic Command. Though Tisbury may be the busy hub of life with its railway station, its tumbling streets and little shops, Hindon is the spiritual mecca. Artists love Hindon too: 'We're a very arty crafty lot here; there must be seven or eight serious painters in the village,' says Brian Kendall, a local landscape artist. The old Methodist church is now selling vegetable dyes to the artistic, who abound in cottages and farmhouses on the breathtakingly beautiful Fonthill estate and in the folds of the hills around.

Hindon used to be an important little town famous for the manufacture of silk twist and for its fairs and markets. In 1754 'a very melancholy fire happened at Hindon', wrote a stone mason called Basil Bevis in a letter a few years later, 'which consumed upwards of one hundred and forty houses'. It began at Mr Tyler's, a cutler: a spark flew from his forge on to the thatch and within four hours, on a hot summer's day in July, two thirds of the town was razed to the ground.

In spite of the fire, however, Hindon rose from the ashes a new town. Rather than growing organically like most villages whose streets curl this way and that, Hindon was rebuilt as a Georgian set piece on a gentle incline. It looks terrifically French, for down its wide formal stretch there are rows of pollarded lime trees which were planted to commemorate the marriage of Edward VII and Alexandra. Many of the houses are built of the local Chilmark stone – the pale, almost chalk-white limestone which makes the area so exceptional. At the top of the street a late-Victorian church looks comfortable and prosperous and is full of newly and brightly tapestried kneelers and lavish flower arrangements. As you walk down the street you can look through archways between the houses and get glimpses of lush gardens or fields of sheep beyond. At the end of the slope, on a mild rise, stands an exremely incongruous house just above the Victorian village hall. It is sad that a house in such commanding position was allowed to be built in mock-Cotswold stone.

'Hindon is a delightful little village, so rustic and pretty amidst its green swelling downs, with great woods crowning the heights beyond, that one can hardly credit the fact that it was formerly an important market and session town and a Parliamentary borough returning two members . . .' So wrote W. H. Hudson when he was staying at the Lamb Inn in 1909 writing his book *A Shepherd's Life*. The Lamb has long been the centre of life in Hindon, for although the village saw its full glory in the early 1800s, and the coming of the railway to Tisbury in 1859 witnessed its gradual decline as a thriving market town, it never ceased to be a stopping-off place for travellers. It is still as much on the map as it ever was, for Hindon lies at the convergence of eight roads and lanes and, until bypassed by the wide slicing ribbon of the A303, it was on the main road between London and the West Country and provided post-horses for coaches. Once the centre of many market-day business transactions; the Lamb is still bustling and alive on any day of the week. Against its bar lean a good mixture of farmers, gamekeepers, artists and retired colonels. At lunch the other day I heard a good ten-minute conversation between a retired General and a young girl with a Mini Metro who was wanting to drive to Winchester.

'Put it like this,' he said, 'you could take the 303 and then branch off through the Teffonts to Salisbury, then you take the A272 . . .'

Right: The Savage monument, Elmley Castle.

Below: Ely Cathedral.

Right: Great Farmcote.

Above: The village smithy, Ford.

Above: Church of St. Mary and All Saints, Fotheringhay

Above: Rosamund's Bower, Manor Farm, Frampton on Severn.

Above: The Chinese bridge, Godmanchester.

Above: Helmingham Hall.

Top left: Rievaulx Abbey, near Helmsley.

Bottom left: Heydon Hall.

Right: Farmland in north-west Herefordshire.

Below: The Lamb at Hindon.

Above: Houghton Hall.

Left: Carving of William Morris in Kelmscott village.

Above: Kiftsgate Court

Above: The Eller Beck, Linton.

Below: East Dean in the Lavant valley.

Left: Church of St John the Evangelist, Little Gidding.

Below: McLeods, Louth.

I don't agree,' she said. 'I think it's far quicker to beetle up to Andover . . .'

At this point a third person butted in, longing to display his topographical knowledge.

There has always been, and there always be, travel talk in the Lamb, just as there will always be 'Long before you were born' stories. Monday night is British Legion night, when old farmers and military men tell stories about the war. What a far cry from when Silas White, a notorious smuggler and leader of the Wiltshire Moonrakers, made the Lamb the centre of his activities. The cellars provided an excellent hiding place for contraband, and in 1954 several blocked-up passages were discovered running parallel to the street.

HOUGHTON HALL

Norfolk

HOUGHTON is a humdinger of a house. It has been virtually untouched inside or out since it was built in the 1720s, and if ever there was unwrecked England it is here. There is an air of loneliness and privacy about the place, as though it had been kept secret from the world, guarded by its great wide park where white deer graze and avenues lead to endless horizons, and by rookeries in the woods all around.

Norfolk is never as flat as in the imagination. Each time I visit it, it undulates more. Beyond Houghton's verdant park, huge cornfields of bright brown earth roll gently out of the sound of the sea and the narrow ribbons of road cut between wide grass verges which once were drove roads. The ancient, dead-straight Peddar's Way track crosses over and over the winding ways to Houghton from Sedgeford and Snettisham, Anmer and Hillington, Flitcham and Grimston. Lines of summer-holidaying families in hot, full cars crowd the main roads to Hunstanton and Cromer, longing for the sea, little knowing what they are passing by a village or two away. The trees begin to abound at Bunkers Hill two miles away from Houghton and turn into serious woods at Blackground. Even if you have seen the Hall before, your pulse quickens at the last bend in the road before the great iron gates of the house are upon you.

The Walpoles had been living at Houghton for nearly 600 years when Sir Robert Walpole, the first prime minister of England, was born. It was he who built this discreetly beautiful, pale-faced Palladian palace which was, and still is, the largest house in Norfolk. The original designs were prepared by Colin Campbell in 1721, but Sir Robert then employed Thomas Ripley, a Yorkshireman who was said to have walked to London to seek his fortune. He started work as a carpenter and ended by succeeding Grinling Gibbons as 'chief carpenter to the King's works'.

Houghton was his first architectural job and he built the Admiralty two years later. Campbell had designed towers for the corners of the house but Walpole, who wanted to out-swank his contemporaries, asked for cupolas. He certainly wasn't going to have his house built of brick – the only material going in Norfolk. Ripley suggested the extravagant measure of using stone from Yorkshire to face the house. It was quarried near Whitby and brought down by boat to King's Lynn. The result was spectacular; Houghton became a star.

The small village, which once surrounded the Jacobean house where Walpole was born, was razed to the ground to provide a fashionably clean sweep of unadulterated parkland in all directions. The villagers were rehoused in neat rows of double cottages (now whitewashed) outside the main gates. Though they may look quaint now, at the time it must have felt like complete devastation. The 'Sweet Auburn' of Oliver Goldsmith's *The Deserted Village*, which decries this eighteenth-century habit of razing villages and rebuilding sanitized rows of cottages out of sight and sound of the mansion, is said by some to have been written about Houghton. Walpole openly disliked Goldsmith, who had described him and his like as complacent, 'At pleasure's lordly call, watching a smiling long-frequented village fall'.

If Walpole's heart was hard, his eye was faultless. Apart from spotting the talents of the untried or tested Ripley, he gave William Kent his first big architectural job. Most of Houghton's ceilings, mouldings, doors, state beds, tables and chairs are designed by the great man and remain in the house. There isn't a palace in the land as grand as Houghton. Walpole's collection of pictures was legendary but, after his death, it was sold to Catherine of Russia in order to pay the debts of his grandson, the third Earl of Oxford, who had let the estate run to rack and ruin.

After Sir Robert's demise Houghton was seldom so cherished

again. It has never changed hands but it has often lain empty, for when male heirs ran out and the Cholmondeleys came into Houghton through the female line, they favoured their estate in Cheshire. Houghton was hardly used in the nineteenth century. It was offered to the Duke of Wellington, who preferred Strathfield Saye, and later to Edward VII, who bought Sandringham instead. Poor Houghton – nobody liked it. Horace Walpole, Sir Robert's second son, hated it: 'In the days when all my soul was tuned to pleasure and vivacity, I hated Houghton and all its solitude; Houghton I know not what to call it, a monument or ruin!' Without Sir Robert's magic hand, Houghton became a melancholy place. In 1913, however, it was revitalized by the fifth Marquess of Cholmondeley and his wife, who lived there for over fifty years and lavished pictures and love on it.

Houghton still has a faint air of melancholy when the rooks caw in the evenings. The small church in the park, its tower built by Sir Robert, houses no monument to the creator of the acres of beauty outside. Only his forefathers lie there peacefully, as well as the disgruntled Horace.

KELMSCOTT MANOR

Oxfordshire

KELMSCOTT MANOR is well hidden. There is no huge brown sign with a doll's-house logo heralding the house on the M4 motorway, nor is there any signpost indicating that a 'heritage site' is near at hand to ease the minds of helpless EC members. You have to find your own way to Kelmscott with a map or by asking how to get there in Lechlade.

The peaceful village lies across willowy meadowland on the Oxfordshire side of the upper Thames. Its houses and cottages are built in the local pale-golden limestone, as is the 'manor', an unassuming sixteenth-century farmhouse. It was built by the Turner family, who farmed the surrounding land for three centuries, adding a wing in the 1670s. In 1871 they let it to William Morris and Dante Gabriel Rossetti.

As you wind down the narrow lane, past the Plough Inn, there are no car parks or toilet signs. The glorious gabled manor, glimpsed first above the secretive garden wall, does not flaunt itself. It doesn't need to. There is no shop full of nostalgically wrapped soap, tasteful tea towels and scented drawer lines, merely a solid oak table just inside the front door where you can buy several books on William Morris, six different postcards and a guide to Kelmscott. The latter is beautifully set out with a frontispiece from *News from Nowhere* (Kelmscott Press, 1892), drawn by Charles Gere. It is of the east front of Kelmscott, where you enter.

Although the inside of the house may not be exactly as it was in the 1870s when Morris, the craftsman, poet, manufacturer and socialist, was designing the 'Willow Bough' wallpaper, writing *The Haystack in the Floods*, and watching his wife Jane fall in love with Rossetti, the atmosphere is still filled with these three pre-

Raphaelites, their friends, and generations of Turners before them. The furnishings are hand-woven, the furniture hand-hewn. The sixteenth-century part of the house is rambling and small roomed; the seventeenth-century addition is more open and elegant with Renaissance fireplaces and Georgian panelling.

Everywhere you look there are paintings by Rossetti, tiles by William de Morgan, embroidered curtains by Jane, wallhangings by Morris and richly decorated Kelmscott Press books. It does not feel in the least like a museum and when you look from a bedroom window to the river Thames meandering down from Lechlade towards Oxford, it isn't hard to imagine William Morris seeing this house as he did for the first time, having arrived by boat:

> Through the hawthorn sprays I could see the flat country spreading out far away under the sea of the calm evening, till something that might be called hills, with a look of sheep pastures about them, bounded it with a soft blue line. Before me, the elm boughs still hid most of what houses there might be in this river-side dwelling of men; but to the right of the cart-road a few grey buildings of the simplest kind showed here and there . . . We crossed the road, and again, almost without my will, my hand raised to the latch of a door, and we stood presently on a stone path which led up to the old house.'

It's a hard place to leave, for it is one of the most peaceful houses I have ever been in, but you can always linger on the way back and look at the Ernest Gimson cottage, built for May Morris, William's daughter, in 1915, and the memorial cottages designed by Philip Webb for Mrs Morris in 1902. There is a stone relief on the front carved by George Jack from a sketch by his friend and partner Webb. The village hall was also designed by Ernest Gimson.

Last of all, call in at the church of St George: in the cemetery, hidden behind a large bay tree, is the grave of William, Jane, Jenny, and May Morris, marked by a coped stone which was also designed by Philip Webb.

KIFTSGATE COURT

Gloucestershire

APART from Sissinghurst, the garden at Hidcote in Gloucestershire is held up as the paragon. It was created from scratch by Lawrence Johnson from the 1900s onwards and unfolds into a series of secret rooms enclosed by spectacular hedges, or pleached trees with sudden glimpses of vistas of distant countryside. The National Trust, which owns it, has well over two million members and sometimes you feel as though most of them are there as you struggle from one hedged room to another in crushed cocktail party circumstances. Hidcote has become a place of automatic pilgrimage, like Stonehenge, and I do not want to go there any more. Its atmosphere has long been dying. This is not the garden's fault; it is still beautiful and it is still exemplarily maintained, but it has no singular and passionate spirit behind it and the devouring eyes of the crowds have somehow stolen its magic.

Down the road, towards the edge of Glyde Hill, is Kiftsgate Court amidst a glorious demense. If Hidcote is Stonehenge then Kiftsgate is Avebury. Its garden may no longer be *secret* but it has retained its mystery and its magic. The situation is startling. The house hovers on the very edge of a steep, partly wooded escarpment like a glider about to take off across the wide Vale of Evesham. The Malverns, twenty miles away, are in the middle distance and on a clear day the outline of the Welsh hills emerges from the blue on the far horizon. Kiftsgate hangs high above the small village of Mickleton. In the mid eighteenth century the owner of Mickleton Manor, Walwyn Graves, had the poet and landscape gardener William Shenstone to stay; he suggested planting an avenue of limes straight up the hill to where Kiftsgate Court now stands. He also suggested planting Scots pines along the top of the escarpment so that the effect from below would be suitably dramatic. In the 1890s Walwyn's descendant, Sydney Graves Hamilton, fired with the Victorian pioneering spirit and a desire for mountain air, decided to build a house at the top of the avenue and that is how Kiftsgate Court came about. He denuded the manor of its eighteenth-century pedimented portico and stuck it on to the front of his new house, which boasted a gigantic ballroom with a sprung floor.

In 1918 the present owner's grandparents, the Muirs, bought Kiftsgate and started a garden from virtually nothing. There was a formal paved area directly in front of the portico and the first thing Heather Muir did was to make some steps leading down from it to a lawn below. Then she was away, making walk after border after summerhouse, with the help and wisdom of a lifelong friend, Major Johnson, her great gardening neighbour from Hidcote. By the early fifties Kiftsgate was on the garden map. Arthur Hellyer wrote in *Gardening*, 'Each rose bush has grown to its maximum proportions and to the conventional gardener will come as a revelation.' The particular pocket of soil upon which Kiftsgate sits has something in it which makes plants, shrubs and trees develop an inexplicable luxuriance.

Perhaps that gift of gardening magic fired Heather Muir's daughter. She took on the garden in the sixties and went on creating. Up and over the escarpment, steps twist and turn between soaring great trees, and shrubs tumble down and down to the sheltered plateau below. In 1983 she wrote, 'I spend many happy and contented hours gardening on my own, stopping now and then to relax with a cigarella . . .' Today her daughter Mrs Chambers tends the garden and talks of it with a breathless enthusiasm. 'This year the roses are just incredible and everything is better than ever, the Kiftsgate rose is stunning.'

In mid July the spectacular Kiftsgate rose is *au point*. In 1938 Heather Muir bought what she thought was a *Rosa moscata*, which thrived unhindered during the war and continued to grow ever more rampantly until it was patently obvious that it was *not* a *Rosa moscata*. In 1951 the rose expert Graham Thomas deemed it unidentifiable and it was officially named *Rosa filipes 'Kiftsgate'*. It is the largest rose in England and winds 50 feet up into a copper beech tree; in places it is nearly 100 feet wide. The *Dictionary of Roses* entry for 'Kiftsgate' reads, 'It is superb, cascading down in great white showers, and no other rose can surpass it.' If the house and garden should ever fall into decay the rose will seize its chance and take over.

THE LAVANT VALLEY

Sussex

AWAY from the coast, there is mile upon mile of unwrecked Sussex. Unlike Surrey, which turns submissively towards London or Kent and is sometimes so tidy that you want to mess it up, parts of Sussex have remained relatively untamed and free from uniformity. It has always been a prosperous county – 'God Bless the sensitive stockbrokers of West Sussex', wrote Ian Nairn in *Buildings of England*. Behind these tracts of unspoiled countryside and pretty villages there are healthy bank balances and articulate inhabitants who know people in high places and how to lobby against possible despoliation, and who sometimes choose good architects for new buildings.

The village of East Dean is unwrecked. Even its service station is good looking and the small community it serves has not yet demanded a canopy, or food shops and chrysanthemum bouquets to go with its petrol. The scale is right for the small and satisfactory village that sits so comfortably in this sequestered, sumptuous Sussex valley below the scarp of the South Downs. Most of the houses and cottages are of flint with brick dressings – typical local materials – and the difficult art of knapping and building with flints is beautifully displayed in the winding lanes leading away from the village green and pond.

Past the pebbledashed Non-Conformist chapel and the Hurdlemakers pub is the friendly flint-faced church of All Saints. There are wide mown paths through its graveyard; the rest is left to grow wild and in consequence boasts nearly a hundred different plants and flowers. The swathe is cut in August and is far more fetching than the closely trimmed and cropped graveyards around most of our churches. Inside there is a hand-written poem in praise of some redundant bell clappers. (Is this where the phrase 'clapped out' comes from?) It was written by the great playwright Christopher Fry, who lives in a cottage in the village.

> These clappers gave the bells their tongue
> And now in quiet here are hung
> But may our voices always sing
> Thy praise, in love continuing.

The best view of the Lavant valley is from the elegant stand at Goodwood racecourse by Arup Associates. From under its tent-like white canopies this chalk kingdom of open, rolling downland is spread below, with bush-scattered combes and cornfields running up into thick, rich beech woods. There is a forgotten track to the east of the racecourse which leads past the woods of Charlton Park and steeply down to the plain rose-bricked perfection of Fox Hall, and then on into the small village of Charlton.

The track was used by Charles the second Duke of Richmond, to hunt the famous Charlton pack of hounds. He tired of riding the two miles from home in the morning and in 1730 he commissioned Lord Burlington to design a perfect mini Palladian palace, consisting of one magnificent gilded room on the first floor with an arched alcove for his bed, space for the servants on the ground floor and a front door leading into the stable yard.

In the pediment above the mantelpiece is an indicator which shows the direction of the wind, important information for the foxhunter. For nearly a hundred years the Charlton Hunt was the most famous and fashionable in the country. It was founded in the 1670s by the Duke of Monmouth, who vowed that if he became king he would keep his court at Charlton. After his death, the Duke of Bolton took over the hunt, but the next duke was lured away from hunting by the famous Lavinia Fenton, the original Polly Peachum of *The Beggars' Opera* and the Duke of Richmond (Charles II's grandson) took charge. The hunt's most famous run was on 26 Janauary 1738, when a fox was found in East Dean Wood at 8.15 in the morning and the hounds ran zigzagging all over the downs until 5.50 in the evening by which time the Duke of Richmond was on his fifth horse, having lamed three. The hunt was finally wound up in 1815 and, apart from the name of Charlton's pub – the Fox – there are few clues to the area's sporting past.

At the church in Singleton, the exceptionally pretty flint village along the valley to the west, there is, however, a memorial eulogizing Thomas Johnson, the eighteenth-century huntsman who was said to have no equal. It was erected by a handful of aristocrats 'in memory of a good and faithful servant, as a reward to the deceased, and an incitement to the living. "Go, and do thou likewise." (St Luke, 10:37)':

> Here Johnson lies; What human can deny
> Old honest Tom the tribute of a sigh?
> Deaf's the ear which caught the opening sound;
> Dumb the tongue which sheer'd the hills around,
> Unpleasing troth; Death hunts us from our birth
> In view, and men, like foxes, take to earth.

LINTON AND THORPE

Yorkshire

THE neighbouring villages of Thorpe-sub-Montem and Linton-in-Craven are as good as you could get in all England. Although they are in perhaps the most beautiful of Yorkshire dales, Wharfedale, to which city dwellers in search of clean air come flocking fom Leeds, Harrogate and Bradford to find oases of solitude at weekends, they have remained unwrecked, ordinary working villages.

Wind up Wharfedale, where the wondrous river Wharfe spreads its waters over boulders into wide shallow pools with sandy beaches. Sometimes it tumbles between rocks, as at the Strid, a 10-foot-wide gorge (over which my husband once jumped while I screamed), where the river narrows into fierce white water, thirty feet deep.

Past Burnsall, a large and beautiful village – settled with a sense of complete belonging into a tree-sprinkled bowl of the hills – the dale widens out, crisscrossed with myriad stone walls. A tiny lane leads off towards the looming Raven Nest Crags, Kail Hill, and Elbolton Hill where, a hundred years ago in a cave below the summit, the remains of bears, wolves, boars and humans were found. The lane loops down between silvery walls of large rounded stones stacked above eye level. No lorry could ever squeeze through to the tiny lost hamlet of Thorpe-in-the-Hollow, as it is sometimes called, enveloped in these cushions of hills. It feels as utterly secret today as it did when it was used for hiding stock and dalesmen from marauders. Thorpe has long been known as the 'hidden hamlet', for it escaped, the depredations of the fourteenth-century Scottish raiders who passed down the dale missing it completely.

Round the last bend you come upon the handsomest classical eighteenth-century farmhouse imaginable, roses stuffed into its front garden and with raggle-taggle barns and farm buildings around it.

Two chained-up sheep dogs wag their tails outside their tin-barrel kennels, a broken-down David Brown tractor waits to be mended on the verge and two clipped lollipop holly trees stand sentinel either side of a cottage gate, as high as the roof. The people of Thorpe were famous shoemakers and supplied the monks at Fountains Abbey. Until fifty years ago a shoemaker lived in a cottage on the lane which peters out into a track and a moorland path; the second lane leads to Thorpeland and Cracoe; the third back on to the road for Linton.

Linton is a different cup of tea, altogether, set in a wide, open stretch of land a little further up the dale. There was once a lake here, and the people of Linton grew flax around it, from which they made linen – hence its name. Stone houses and cottages are spread around a generous and irregularly shaped green through which the Eller Beck flows. Thirty brown ducks and one white Pecking waddle around in a busy group. A clapper bridge, a packhorse bridge and stepping stones cross this way and that under tall beech trees and sycamores. There is a manor house and farm, two rectories, a post office, a yeoman's house and a pub called the Black Sheep. It is a loved village, but without a hint of self-conscious conservation about it – it is not tarted up, or over-restored, or twee, but reserved and unflashy.

Except, that is, for the grandest set of almshouses in all England which dominate one side of the green. They were founded by Richard Fountaine, who was born in Linton in 1639 and became a London timber merchant during the time when timber was in great demand during the Plague and Fire of London. He made a fortune and when he died at the age of eighty-one he left money for a mini Castle Howard to be built of millstone grit from Thorpe Fell. It provides six cottages and a chapel in the centre which is, at the moment of writing, being beautifully restored by English Heritage. There is argument as to whether the architect Vanbrugh designed the building or not. I should think he did, for he designed an identical set of almshouses for his parish in London but they were never built. He also used Fountaine as his timber merchant.

LITTLE GIDDING

Huntingdonshire

Midwinter spring is its own season
Sempiternal though sodden towards sundown,
Suspended in time, between pole and tropic.
When the short day is brightest, with frost and fire,
The brief sun flames the ice, on pond and ditches,
In windless cold that is the heart's heat,
Reflecting in a watery mirror
A glare that is blindness in the early afternoon.

AND if you come to the tiny church of St John the Evangelist at Little Gidding in midwinter, as T. S. Eliot describes, you will be rewarded. It is in an obscure and isolated piece of countryside, where flattish, watery pastures, wide-verged roads, low hedges and distant pylons abound. Farms stand on mild rises. Little Gidding floats between the level, zigzag-drained Fens to the east and the high-hedged, hunting country of Northamptonshire to the west.

To a small hill above the Alconbury brook set between Steeple and Great Gidding, up a long-lost avenue of trees, Nicholas Ferrar made his way in the 1620s. Here he found the decaying manor house of Little Gidding and the abandoned parish church – its nave a barn, its vestry a pig sty. The place was, 'with respect to privacy of situation, exactly suited to his wishes'. His strength of purpose and the small community he founded here, though it lasted only twenty-five years, remain an inspiration to this day. Little Gidding soon became a place of pilgrimage, and one of its more recent pilgrims was T. S. Eliot:

. . . There are other places
Which also are the world's end, some at the sea jaws,
Or over a dark lake, in a desert or a city –

But this is the nearest, in place and time,
Now and in England.

Nicholas Ferrar was born in London in 1592, the son of a founder of the Virginia Company, set up to colonize the New World. His rapid grasp of Greek and Latin enabled him to go to Clare College, Cambridge, at the age of fourteen. As a child he had suffered from sudden high fevers, but at Cambridge they became so bad that he was advised by his doctor to spend some time abroad. He attended the universities of Leipzig in Germany and Padua in Italy, where he studied medicine for two years. He acquired a knowledge of High Dutch, Italian, French and Spanish and in 1618 he returned to England, where he was offered an academic post in London; he decided instead to join his father's textile business.

Nicholas was the perfect Renaissance man – a fine scholar, a natural leader and a powerful speaker. He set himself the highest standards and his qualities were well known at the court of King James. However, he became increasingly depressed by the world he saw around him. Although he served in Parliament for a brief period and was offered a clerkship to the Privy Council and the British ambassadorship in Savoy, he was saddened by the lack of principles and blatant debauchery and corruption in royal and political circles, and by 1624 had taken the decision to retire from public life and form a religious community.

The village of Little Gidding, to which Nicholas and his mother retreated, had been victim to the Black Death. There were a few shepherds' cottages, and the remains of more. Today the field along which you travel towards the church is probably much as it was then, a series of undulations delineating field systems and the vestiges of a medieval community. The Ferrars put the manor and church in order and in 1626 Nicholas, who had always had mystic leanings, fasted for eight weeks, after which he was ordained a deacon. A new way of life began at Little Gidding. With the arrival of Nicholas's brother and his wife, children, relations and tutors, the group grew to about forty. They had three services a day and were in close contact with the poet George Herbert, who lived at the neighbouring village of Leighton Bromswold. The women of the group made the most exquisite and now world-famous embroidery, known as *opus little gidding*. They made covers for the pulpit, reading desk, communion table, kneelers and devotional books – blue for Sundays, green for weekdays. Nicholas believed, like Laud, in expressing the 'beauty of holiness' through decorating the church with fine things – the antithesis of the Puritan movement. King Charles I, a High Anglican and married to a Catholic, became very attached to the Ferrar community and its works and visited Little Gidding several times, finally in 1642, only months before the outbreak of civil war.

Nicholas Ferrar died in 1637, but the community continued until it was pillaged and sacked by the Puritans in 1646, the woodwork burnt, the silver claws from the brass eagle lectern gouged out and the rest chucked into the village pond. Nicholas's nephew John renovated the church in 1714, adding the strange stone façade, remaking the panelling and choir stalls and rescuing the brass font and lectern from the mud, all in memory of his visionary uncle.

Today a recently created community has built near the church a wall and pathway of astounding insensitivity and ugliness; they do their utmost to detract from the intensely strong feeling of holiness at Little Gidding. However, the church itself remains utterly inspirational.

> . . . So, while the light fails
> On a winter's afternoon, in a secluded chapel
> History is now and England.

LOUTH

Lincolnshire

LINCOLNSHIRE is maligned and unloved by those who do not know it. 'The second largest county in England and the least appreciated,' wrote Henry Thorold in his Shell Guide to Lincolnshire. 'The book sold better than every other *Shell Guide*, except perhaps *Cornwall*,' he told me, 'not because it was a good book but because nobody else had written about this dim county. When people ask me where I live, and I say 'Lincolnshire', they say, "I don't know the county at all, isn't it particularly dull and flat?" It is neither.

Mercifully for Lincolnshire, no one wants to visit it and whole chunks of it remain unwrecked and aloof from the rest of England, almost like another country. Henry Thorold, who showed me the way to Louth, is also unwrecked. He takes no newspapers, has no wireless or television, but he takes the *Oldie*. We travelled on minor roads through villages with strange names like Boothby Graffoe, whose pubs advertise Bateman's Good Honest Ales, one of the few independent breweries still left in family ownership.

From The Cliff, a long undulating limestone ridge high above the vale, with Lincoln's cathedral rising in the distance like Mont-Saint-Michel from the beach, we crossed the heath, once a wild and desolate place. A lighthouse 150 feet high used to guide people across it. Since the enclosure acts the heath has been tamed, like the Cotswolds, with drystone walls either side of the roads, and we could be in high Gloucestershire as we wind into the ravishing limestone village of Scopwick, with a wide stream running through its midst. 'Lincolnshire's reply to Bourton-on-the-Water,' says Thorold. On we go past modest red-brick Thorpe Tilney Hall, Lincolnshire's answer to Glyndebourne, and down over Blankney Fen beside the great ditch of Timberland Delph to Kirkstead with its ruined abbey and tiny Early English church of St Leonard's.

Woodhall Spa, the golfers' mecca, unfurls its sandy, Scots piney, Sunningdale-like streets which lead past high, red-brick Victorian and Edwardian houses and a huge mock-Tudor golfing hotel, and out into the foothills of the Wolds. Beside the road runs the extinct railway line to the Georgian market town of Horncastle, home of Joseph Banks and bustling with a Saturday market.

The Wolds are empty. Old drove roads with wide, wide verges climb up into great sweeping countryside. The chalk shows white through the plough on distant curves of land and there are clumps of beech trees along the tops. They say that the best road on which to approach Louth is from Hainton and Burgh on Bain. Suddenly and dramatically the church spire cuts into the sky from a gentle fold in the Wolds.

You can enter Louth through Eastgate, Northgate, Westgate, Upgate, Walkergate, Ludgate, Ramsgate, Kidgate, Gospelgate, Cisterngate, or Chequergate. You can also vary the pronunciation of its name from the two-syllabled version, which the locals use – Lou (like Cow) -ath, to the long-drawn-out one-syllabled version, which the old-fashioned gentry use – Lou (like cow)-the; or you can simply say Louth to rhyme with mouth. Whichever way, Louth is one of the best market towns in England – it is up in my top five along with Ludlow, Stamford, Bernard Castle and Devizes. The late Jack Yates, who had a famous bookshop here, referred to the fifties villas on the hillside as you enter the town on the road from the west as 'Beverly Hills'. Just beyond them, hard on the road, is Thorpe Hall, an Elizabethan house with tall clustered chimneys, haunted by the 'Green Lady'. Then, as you curl into Westgate, Louth proper begins – a rose-red town of more shades of beautiful brick and pantiles and more good eighteenth-century houses than you can ever imagine. The brick runs from the palest apricot to the richest crimson, the houses from the grandest William and Mary mansion behind high walls to the neatest Georgian doctor's house behind well-clipped laurel hedges and, in the middle of the winding streets, the contrasting stone church, early sixteenth century, rises elegantly from its grassy clearing. The huge Victorian town hall is described by Thorold as like 'the Vatican in front and a slaughter house behind'. You can enter the nearby covered market under a gaunt and tall Bavarian tower. On the corner is the printing firm of Parkers, who printed Lincolnshire's famous son Tennyson's first book of poems.

Almost the best thing of all is that Louth is full of *proper* shops. They are shops I have never heard of: instead of McDonald's there is Ron-de-Vou's café; instead of W. H. Smith there is Spencers bookshop; and instead of Sainsbury's there are two of the best grocers in the county, Larders and Mcleods – the latter, in Upgate beside the church and opposite a beautiful apricot-coloured terrace of houses, sells excellent vegetable samosas.

Louth is a winner. Unlike so many English towns which have lost their identities through predictable uniformity, Louth has kept its dignity – and luckily its distance.

LYFORD

Berkshire

THE discreet charm of Lyford is a revelation. It is a tiny village with thirty-eight inhabitants in the Vale of the White Horse which few would think of visiting. It has no pub, and is on the way from nowhere to nowhere in particular, in what might look to some like remarkably dull and flat country. There, on the near horizon, is the long line of Berkshire Downs levelling off into this verdant vale of Old Berks hunting ground. Goosey, three miles west, might appear more picturesque with its wide village green speckled with tethered horses, but few know of the greater, hidden beauty of Lyford.

Although much of this tract of Berkshire countryside (now called Oxfordshire) is easily accessible from London and many of the villages around have been daintified to the hilt – cottages with carriage lamps on either side of their front doors groan with over-restoration, front gardens are gravelled over to become car ports, back gardens are stiff with fierce, foreign batallions of cypress leylandii defending their commuting owners' privacy – yet Lyford has remained apart from all this, an untouched rural backwater. Perhaps this is because it has always been in single ownership, which has put paid to piecemeal development. Much of it is now under the auspices of St John's College, Oxford, which bought the village in 1981 from the Moores family (of Littlewoods pools fame), who had in turn bought it from its centuries-old owners, Worcester College, in 1973.

Lyford lies among small, watery meadows through which the river Ock winds its willowy way and a herd of Friesian cows amble home for milking towards Manor Farm. The great-gabled and tall-chimneyed house is seventeenth century. The Pike family, tenants of the college, have farmed the same land here for 300 years and their name occurs on many a headstone in the small yew-encircled graveyard close by. Before the 1700s the Ashcombe family owned the estate and lived at Manor Farm, and it was the public-spirited Oliver who in his will endowed the Lyford almshouses. The original ones were built in the early seventeenth century, with enough money to provide meat, drink and clothing for the aged poor of the village in perpetuity. The present almshouses, however, date from the early eighteenth century.

Today the Oliver Ashcombe Charity is in charge of the six dwellings within the little court. A small committee consisting of four members from the village (Mr Pike the farmer among them), a solicitor whose family has been on the committee for four generations, and an Oxford college bursar, choose who is to live there. On Midsummer's Day every year they hold a tea party at the almshouses for the whole village.

Oliver Ashcombe was a son-in-law of John Yate, who owned the adjoining land and lived at the once-moated Lyford Grange which lies north-east of the village. In 1581 John Yate had harboured the famous Jesuit martyr Edmund Campion, for his house was full of secret hiding places, but on 17 July Campion was captured along with two other priests and taken through a hooting mob, to the Tower of London. He had his elbows tied behind his back, his hands in front, and his legs beneath his horse's stomach; a piece of paper was pinned to his hat saying, 'Campion, the seditious Jesuit'. His unshakeable Papist beliefs and his *Decem Rationes*, which he preached privately, led to his torture and execution.

Lyford's little church of St Mary the Virgin was built almost wholly during the first half of the thirteenth century. The Ashcombe and Yate families erected all their memorials in the mother church at nearby West Hanney, and Lyford's was merely used for a monthly service. During the seventeenth and eighteenth centuries it fell into disrepair, but a Victorian benefactor restored it during a period of fervent religious revival at a cost of £1,000. It is a lovely church, not over-restored, and it retains an ancient and holy atmosphere.

Apart from the excitement of Edmund Campion's arrest, and the shock of a Lancaster bomber crashing in a nearby field in 1945 and breaking all the glass in the village, Lyford has made no headline news, but for a boy prodigy who was born here in 1725 and grew to 5 feet tall by the time he was eight. His father prudently exhibited him to the curious at Reading and made a little money.

MAPPERTON

Dorset

MAPPERTON is one of the best ancient houses in Dorset. There are
other such manors in the area – Bingham's Melcombe, Cranborne,
Parnham, Creech Grange – but for me, Mapperton tips the balance.
It is the combination of its bright golden stone, its spectacular garden
and its breathtaking position 400 feet up in deepest Dorset, where
the silence and feeling of remoteness are absolute.

You can tell this is true country just by ambling through the near-
perfect neighbouring town of Beaminster. There is no proliferation of
off-licences and delicatessens which seem to sprout up in other market
towns, where the indigenous locals have been driven out by *new*
country people paying irresistible prices for their homesteads and
wanting to eat and drink what they are used to. Beaminster is safe.
The drive from London takes three hours – too far for even the most
zealous weekender to swoop on and renovate a cottage and then say,
'You really should have seen the state it was in when we found it.'

The country round Mapperton is like an English Tuscany – small
hills stretching away into the distance – but green, wooded, beloved
and immortalized by Dorset's great pastoral poet William Barnes.
Whether you approach Mapperton from the town below or by
winding up and over from Evershott, its position at the head of a
sudden and secret valley is a complete surprise. You approach the
house, with its outbuildings, like a small hamlet, huddled round it,
down a short straight drive which leads you to the west front. It is
shaped like an E, one side of which is formed by a small chapel; set a
little apart are two ravishing Renaissance stable blocks which
continue the courtyard effect and lead your eye out over a ha-ha to
level fields.

It is only when you walk through to the eastern side of the house that you first glimpse Mapperton's hidden glory: from the plateau on which the house stands a dramatic valley falls steeply away, winding in a long slow curving descent towards thick woods and the unknown pastures of distant Dorset. From the house and down the first slopes of the valley there stretches a magical garden, worth travelling a hundred miles to see. It was created in three completely different stages but rolls into one wonderful whole: like the house, it has evolved over time – the same local stone has been used throughout and topiary yew trees, gradually added over the years, merge the varying dates of building.

At the head of the valley there is an elaborate Italianate garden, created in the 1920s by the then owner, Mrs Labouchère, according to the fashion of the day. Wide, shallow steps lead down between gently banked lawns to terraces of early crazy paving. There are stepped octagonal rose beds, statues, a pond choked with lilies, Roman columns, yew rooms, secret places and an inordinate number of stone storks. One huge step below is the seventeenth-century terrace where an Elizabethan garden house looks down on to two oblong carp ponds. Below this is the latest garden of shrubs and trees which was started by Victor Montagu in the 1950s and is still being added to by his son and daughter-in-law. Through young woodland a path wanders on and on down the valley and eventually doubles back, zigzagging upwards. You will have walked half a mile if you complete the circuit back to the house.

Until this century Mapperton had a long history of unbroken occupation and continuous descent – from the family of Brett or Bryte, who owned the manor in the time of Edward I, to the Morgans, Brodrepps and Comptons, each inheriting through the female line. Robert Morgan of Mapperton was granted a licence by Henry IV to sit in his presence with a hat on because of 'diverse infirmities which he hath in his hedde and cannot convenintly, without his great daungier, be discovered of the same'. His grandson Robert built the present house in the middle of the sixteenth century, but it has since had the layers of time laced in and around it and it is much changed from the original. Richard Brodrepp built the exquisite stable ranges and joined the original Tudor house to the church in the seventeenth century, and the fourth and last Richard Brodrepp classicized the north front in the eighteenth.

When I left Mapperton I could not resist travelling on down the valley by the ancient track – long abandonded as a drive. It ranks as one of the top ten tracks in the whole of England, winding for over a mile through lost parkland and on beside a stream past a ruined mill, past clumps of yellow flags and patches of bright pink vetch until it eventually reaches the road to North Poorton.

MAUD HEATH'S CAUSEWAY

Wiltshire

THE path known as Maud Heath's Causeway is a wonder – it is not 'waymarked' by the Countryside Commision, but leads simply and quietly for four and a half miles beside the small road between Langley Burrell and Bremhill. A sundial on a beautiful stone pillar erected in 1698 heralds the causeway of sixty-four brick arches rising over what were once the mud flats of the wide river Avon, and praises the great lady who is said to have made her fortune by selling eggs which she carried in a basket once a week to Chippenham market. Carved on the column are the words, 'To the memory of the worthy Maud Heath of Langley Burrell widow, who in the year of grace 1474, for the good of travellers did in charity bestow in land and houses about eight pounds a year forever to be laid out on the highways and causeway leading from Wick Hill [near Bremhill] to Chippenham Clift [near Langley Burrell].' The charity still maintains the path.

Although Langley Burrell sounds like the name of a newsreader on Channel Four, it is in fact a pretty village of widely spaced cottages, a good Early English, Perpendicular and Decorated church, a dullish Georgian manor house and a lovely seventeenth-century parsonage of honey-coloured stone with a perfect doll's-house façade of 1730. Here lived the famous diarist Parson Kilvert, whose family had long belonged to the village. He returned to become the incumbent in 1872, and wrote in October of that year, '. . . round the quiet church the trees were gorgeous, the elms dazzling golden and the beeches turning crimson. The golden elms illuminated the church and churchyard with strong yellow light and the beeches flamed and glowed scarlet fire like the Burning Bush.'

A side road leads off towards the distant heights of Wick Hill.

Beside the raised causeway stands the simple little eighteenth-century chapel of St Giles, which serves the small hamlet of Kellaways, named after the medieval lords of the manor, and across the wide, flat, floodable fields of linseed stands the small seventeenth-century gabled manor house which is now a farm. In 1878, when John Long was the tenant farmer, the Royal Agricultural Society journal reported, 'This farm has all the requisites of a prize farm . . . we had therefore very great pleasure in awarding first prize (in all England) to Mr Long . . . the arable is cultivated like a garden, being wonderfully free from weeds.'

The path leads on past chestnut trees and munching Jersey cows to hill-sheltered East Tytherton, a ravishing village stretching in three directions from the central and formal green. There is no Church of England church, for it is a Moravian settlement and its good, plain, almost severe Georgian architecture is the creation of those early Moravian followers who came here with their leader John Fenwick in 1742. John Huss had begun the original 'Free Church' movement of evangelical communion in the mid fifteenth century. Persecuted and driven from their native Bohemia, the Moravians took refuge in Saxony on Graf von Zinzendorf's estate. From there they sent missionaries all over the world. At East Tytherton they built a sisters' house, chapel and manse for the minister, and a handsome girls' boarding school which was in operation until 1936 and which Kilvert's mother attended. Old girls still return for an annual get-together. Mrs Archard, who lives in the village and comes from four generations of Moravians, has a friend who always takes a taxi the thirty miles from Salisbury and has not missed a year yet. There are several other practising Moravians in the village and their minister serves three parishes, including Swindon and Malmesbury. There are churches in Bath, Bristol and London, and a strong concentration in Yorkshire around Pudsey.

Before leaving the village do not miss Mr Baker's garden on the corner. He has lived here for sixty years and (at the time of writing) there could hardly be a better front garden in the land. It is stuffed with sumptuous bedding plants in summer and by autumn his decorative varieties of dahlia are just coming into their own – scarlet, orange and crimson. Travel up the steep hill, past two idyllic thatched cottages with well-kempt gardens, until you reach the great stone column set in a lumpy field of ragwort from which Maud Heath, with her bonnet and basket, surveys the wide, wide fifty-mile view of the high-hedged, well-treed Avon vale. A stark line of chalk downland stretches out on the horizon behind her. Although the monument looks like the work of Eric Gill, it was in fact erected in 1838 by the glamorous Henry, Marquess of Landsdowne, who became Chancellor of the Exchequer at twenty-five, and that great poet, divine and antiquary, the Vicar of Bremhill, William Lisle Bowles. His poem inscribed on the base of the column reads,

> Thou who dost pause on this aerial height
> Where Maud Heath's Pathway winds in shade or light
> Christian wayfarer in a world of strife
> Be still and ponder on the Path of Life.

THE PETO GARDENS

Iford, Wiltshire

Here in a deep valley where the river Frome flows by, dividing Somerset from Wiltshire, lies one of the secret wonders of the West Country. A fifteenth-century bridge, built by the monks of Hinton Charterhouse, leads to the idyllic manor house which Harold Ainsworth Peto found in 1899 like a 'sleeping beauty' and where he decided to create the garden of a lifetime. A bold statue of Britannia, erected by Peto, stands in the middle of the bridge and demonstrates this unusual gardener's genius for creating magic through incongruity.

Peto had enjoyed a successful architectural partnership with Sir Ernest George and together, in the 1880s, they had built a startling sequence of Dutch-looking houses in Harrington Gardens in London, one of which was for W. S. Gilbert. An admirer of their work, Edwin Lutyens, joined the firm as an apprentice when he was eighteen until he struck out on his own. By the end of the century Peto became increasingly interested in garden design and created gardens around great English houses such as Buscot Park in Oxfordshire and at grand villas in the South of France. Iford, his own garden, remains his masterpiece.

He restored the rambling ancient back regions of the house to accord with William Morris's ideal of medieval tranquillity, retaining the grander eighteenth-century formality at the front. The Romans, who had a knack for choosing perfect building sites, had been here long before, and the fact that there have been people living on this actual spot for nearly 2,000 years gives Iford an unusually settled feel. For Peto, it was 'A Haunt of Ancient Peace' and he immediately embarked on a manuscript which he called, in true Medieval Revival style, *The Boke of Iford*.

He believed that for the highest development of beauty a garden must contain both architecture and plants. 'Old buildings of masonry', he wrote, 'carry one's mind back to the past in a way that a garden of flowers only cannot do. Gardens that are too stony are equally unsatisfactory; it is a combination of the two in just proportion which is the most satisfactory.' So he proceeded to bring a corner of Italy into this far corner of Wiltshire. It was an extremely eccentric thing to do in what was already a garden of Eden, but it works. The surprise of it takes your breath away.

It is as far from the *beau idéal* of an English country garden as you can get. No quaint, haphazard rectory flowerbeds for Peto: 'It is difficult to understand', he said, 'what pleasure anyone can derive from the ordinary herbaceous border . . . without the slightest attempt at form, and the taller plants tied in a shapeless truss to a stake, and the most discordant colours huddled together.' He thought that the picture should be painted with hedges, canals, broad walks, with seats and statues and tall cypresses, and that the flowers were 'entirely subordinate'.

For thirty years Peto built his dream on this steep tumbling hillside. When he first came, there were a series of grass terraces rising above the house and ending in a long, hanging wood, where now the King Edward VII column towers among the trees and commands the valley view. For years before, Peto had been an assiduous and discerning collector of ancient objects and here at last was the perfect setting. From the hanging wood a long flight of steps leads down on to the Great Terrace, which is like a triumphal way paved with stone and lined on one side with a series of Ionic columns. Two oil jars shipped from Nice stand on either side of the steps; according to Peto, they were '. . . the largest I have ever seen. They arrived so damaged by their long journey that I had to put copper bands and rivets to hold them together.' Along the length of the terrace are set bay trees in tubs, lions on plinths, a Greek sarcophagus, and the eastern end is stopped by a seventeenth-century garden house which was moved from another site.

The gardens are full to the brim with Peto's trophies languishing in cool colonnades and arbours, beside fountains and ponds, on pedestals and in niches. He believed that the French masons of the thirteenth and fourteenth centuries had reached the summit of the Gothic spirit, and bought pieces which had come indirectly from the clerk of works in charge of the restoration of Reims Cathedral. Perhaps his *pièce de résistance* is the cloisters, built in the Italian romanesque style, using stone from a nearby disused bridle path. Thirteenth-century lions from Lombardy guard the entrance and inside there is a little court containing fragments from Greece, Italy and France.

PRIDEAUX PLACE

Cornwall

PRIDEAUX PLACE looks out over castellated garden walls and turrets to a deer park which slopes down into the Camel estuary and across to the sand duney country around Bray Hill and beyond. Like most Elizabethan houses it is on a road, small and unimportant now, which turns into a rambling farm track in one direction and leads steeply down into the small town and fishing port of Padstow in the other. Prideaux Place has a reserved and gentle air, and a feeling of deep quietude about it – a welcome peace after the aggressive cacophony of Rock, Cornwall's answer to Cowes.

It is from Rock that you can take the ferry to get here. On a breezy, sunny summer's day it teems with assured and bossy people going out or coming back from sailing. They are noiser than any other group of people I have ever encountered and utterly intolerant of non-sailors. They carry pieces of unrecognizable equipment from cars to boats or vice versa and shout to their children, 'For Gods' sake hurry up', and call to their dogs 'Noodle' and 'Toblerone' in shrill, impatient tones. In the background is the tinkering sound of wire plunging against masts like nautical violins, while slack sails flap loudly. Everyone appears to know exactly what they are doing, which makes you feel at once envious, inadequate and paranoid. It is a blessed relief to climb into the ferry and get to Padstow, awash with ordinary people buying ice creams.

You walk round the harbour of slate-hung houses, past souvenir and false flower shops, past the small, ancient abbey house of glistening granite with madonna lilies on its balcony, past tarted-up trippery pubs, and thread your way through to a back street which, as it ascends the hill, grows empty and quiet. Georgian and Victorian houses with geraniums stuffed in their front windows line the way towards the gigantic ilex and beech trees which secrete Prideaux Place from the town.

As you turn the corner and walk under the trees, there is the house on a wide grassy plateau, open to the public as discreetly as could be. There is hardly a sign up – it is almost as though the Prideaux family has just left the door open for you to walk in. The house is built of the local rag slate which over the centuries has been smothered in the palest lichens.

Various members of the family have impressed their fashionable mark on Nicholas's original E-shaped house of the late sixteenth century – most notably Edmund, who returned from the Grand Tour in 1739 full of romantically classical ideas, built temples in the garden and Georgianized the windows. The next radical change came with the Reverend Charles Prideaux, who gave the house a Regency Gothic veneer at the beginning of the nineteenth century and transformed some of its chief rooms into Strawberry Hill Gothic confections. He left the hall alone. It still has extraordinarily rich and beautiful Elizabethan and eighteenth-century panelling, and he didn't even know about the wonderful ceiling of the great chamber, which has only just been uncovered and will knock your socks off. I gaped.

There are some exceptional Art Nouveau light switches – the house was the first in Cornwall to have electricity (perhaps this is why one of the present Prideaux dogs is called 'Light-bulb'). In the drawing room there is an amusing picture of four Prideaux daughters and their companion, Miss Shaugnessy, rowing a boat through a storm towards the 'doom bar' in the estuary on their way to rescue two men from a shipwreck. They were awarded the Silver Medal of Bravery in 1878.

A large sunken garden, lost in the undergrowth, has just been restored to glory with the voluntary help of the Cornwall Gardens Trust, the National Trust and others. It was an exemplary venture – few historic house-owners can afford to fund such projects, let alone keep their houses in reasonable repair. It remains for the government to reform the tax system to take account of the maintenance of historic houses – the situation at the moment is mad and illogical.

Walk under the ornamental bridge beside some of the best walls in England, built of wafer-thin feathery rag slate set upright in tight packed rows, bursting with ferns and valerian, and then branch off down a path called Trictroll across stubble fields and round back to Padstow. Or you can continue on along the farm track, where a lot of wild mint grows on the banks, towards Tregirls Farm and beach: the full view of the estuary and the open sea will astound you. Here is miles of beautiful coast, unwrecked, unadulterated and *not* owned by the National Trust.

RAME

Cornwall

IF YOU approach Rame along the wooded valley of the river Liner and dip and twist through the village of Millbrook, you can take a narrow lane either by way of the tiny hamlet of Wiggle or through an even smaller place called Forder, straddling a stream. From hilltops and at the end of sudden valleys are glimpses of the sea, ivy hangs from holly trees in the hedges, and acres of bracken, brown now, tumble down the cliffs. You pass a farm where a hanging sign sticks out into the road saying, 'RABBITS – PET OR PLATE'. Travelling on up the cow-muck-spattered lane you see a white stucco farmhouse called Rame Barton set in a jumbled yard. A placard stuck to a tree advertises merely bed and breakfast. Just beyond, where the wonky rubble wall is full of ivy-leaved toadflax, a gate appears leading to the church which serves this tiny hamlet and parish of Rame.

The name means 'high protruding cliff; the ram's head', and the church offers the last shelter before the desolate headland. It is dug deep into the hill to protect it from sea gales. Partly thirteenth century, it is all built of rough slate and has a slender, unbuttressed tower and strange 'broached' spire. Inside, it reveals a double-aisled splendour which is still lit by candles – nothing else. The place feels ancient and cut off from the rest of the world. Its surrounding graveyard is huge, wild and unkempt. The headstones are packed tightly together, for this beautiful place high above the cliffs is a favourite burial place. A simple stone in the porch reads 'E. O. L. GONE HOME'.

Cornwall stands apart from the rest of England, cut off from the Saxons – Celtic to the hilt. Here you feel on the edge of the world. On the very summit of the headland is the small mariners' chapel of St Michael, which is built on the site of an earlier Celtic hermitage. It is a twenty-minute walk from the hamlet of Rame to the chapel. The narrow road passes a row of coastguards' cottages and ends on a blustery bluff beside a radio mast and lookout hut. A path across smooth turf and worn rocks continues steeply down and up again, a daunting route for the faint-hearted. On a winter's day the chapel is a welcome shelter, 300 feet up in the teeth of the wind. The east window, glassless, looks towards Plymouth Sound and to tiny specks of sails miles out to sea. Among countless pieces of graffiti wrought by local lovers, 'I LOVE MANDY' stands out from the rest, carved large and clear into the slate sill. Hawks hover at eye level above the precipitous slopes of bracken, and below them the massive ramparts of cliff drop sheer to the sea where basking sharks lurk.

Earl Ordulf, owner of vast estates in the West Country and uncle of King Ethelred, gave Rame to Tavistock Abbey which he had founded in 981. Over the centuries the land around Rame Head passed to the Dawneys, the Durnfords, the Edgcombes, and finally to Plymouth Council. From the fifteenth century, until the Eddystone Lighthouse was built eight miles off the coast, Plymouth paid a watchman at Rame to maintain a beacon there to warn shipping and to bring the city news of the arrival of important ships.

In 1815 the HMS *Bellerophon*, with its infamous passenger Napoleon, was watched over from Rame while it was anchored in the neighbouring Cawsand Bay for a month. His presence was the talk of Devon and Cornwall. So many dinghies, rafts, barges and skiffs had sailed out to the *Bellerophon*, filled with gawping onlookers, that you could walk from Plymouth Hoe all the way to Cawsand on their decks. Napoleon was finally persuaded to emerge from his cabin, having ordered a new pair of gloves and sent his suit to be pressed in Plymouth: he faced the jeers with dignity. When the crew finally slipped anchor and set sail for St Helena, past Penlee Point, where the foghorn now moans, Rame Head and the Port Eliot and Antony estates along the cliff were the last bit of England he set eyes upon. He turned to Captain Maitland and said quietly, '*Enfin, ce beau pays.*'

RESTORMEL CASTLE

Cornwall

RESTORMEL CASTLE is unwreckable – a perfect Norman stronghold high on a Cornish hill. The natural hilltop has been flattened, and a huge circular moat cut into it, about 60 feet wide and 30 feet deep. Inside is one of the most stalwart and satisfying symmetrical keeps I know. It has not changed since Queen Victoria made an expedition there from Fowey in September 1846. She wrote:

> We got into our own carriage with our ladies, and the gentlemen following in others, and drove through some of the narrowest streets I ever saw in England, it really quite alarmed me. We then drove on for a long way on bad narrow roads, higher and higher up, commanding a fine and very extensive view of the hilly country of Cornwall, its hills covered with fields, and interspersed with hedges. At last we came to one field where there was no road whatsoever, but we went down the hill quite safely, and got out of the carriage at the top of another where, surrounded by woods, stands the circular ruin, covered with ivy, of the old Castle of Restormel, belonging to the Duchy of Cornwall, and in which the Earl of Cornwall lived in the thirteenth century. It is very picturesque. . .

There it stands, as picturesque as ever before the steep, deep valley of the river Fowey, which every so often hums with the noise of the clattering train speeding from Penzance to Paddington. The small road which leads out of Lostwithiel is thick with ferns. A tumbling stream gushes down on to the roadside and where the valley widens the Lostwithiel Bowling Club spreads its verdant lawn under old oak trees. Straight on, the great granite gateposts lead to Restormel Farm with its elegant Gothicized manor below. The pale-brick slate-roofed farm buildings are exceptionally beautiful, and from here a lane winds up between rhododendron bushes towards the perfect castle mound.

The English Heritage signs are so discreet that they are almost invisible. The word 'English' has been sprayed out with a silver aerosol by the Cornish nationalists who feel that this, the terrain of the first earls of Cornwall, is theirs alone. The Fowey valley was dominated throughout the Middle Ages by the castle at Restormel. Once the property of Henry III, it was then passed to his brother Richard, the first Earl of Cornwall, who made it his main residence. He kept his court here and used the 'Trinity' chapel at the foot of the hill, the remains of which still lie under the west wing of the manor house. The 'Earl of Cornwall' continued as a title until Edward III made his seven-year-old son the first and hence the premier, duke in the kingdom. This son became known as the Black Prince, and visitied Restormel many times, but by then it was already falling out of repair. When he was living in Bordeaux he sent orders to John de Kendall, who was in charge of the estate, asking him to send large quantities of 'salt venison and fish and also the pewter plate which we have at Restormel'.

The castle was barely used from the fifteenth century onwards, and became the romantic ruin it is today. In the nineteenth century Mr Masterman, the MP for Bodmin, could not believe his luck when, on marrying an heiress, he found he had inherited the lease of Restormel – its castle, manor and grounds. Being a man of fasionable taste, he landscaped the ancient deer parks surrounding the castle, planting specimen trees such as silver firs, tulip trees, variegated sycamores and turkey oaks. He made paths which wound upwards through woods to the castle. The vestiges of Masterman's romantic leanings can still be seen.

The Duchy of Cornwall, which still own the grounds, is often confused with the county. The Duchy is in fact a large collection of estates, not only within Cornwall but also in Devon, Dorset, Somerset and elsewhere – even in London, for instance. Lostwithiel became the Duchy capital. The revenue from the estates goes to the upkeep of the eldest son of the reigning sovereign, in accordance with Edward III's dictate of 1336.

St Columb Major

Cornwall

IN SUMMER Cornwall's coastal villages and towns are so crowded
with strangers that they become almost unreal and rather like
elaborate film sets. Locals either rent out their houses or hide. St
Columb is not like that at all. It is a few miles inland from Newquay
– far enough away from the cliffs and the huge waves which roll in
from the Atlantic to be given a miss, with the help of a by-pass.

The small hillside town sits beautifully above the river Menathyl,
which winds down the well-wooded Vale of Laherne towards St
Mawgan and the sea. It is one of those 'rich Cornish valleys so much
admired by the inhabitants' wrote Mr Mitton in 1915 in his book,
Cornwall; 'Cornish people go for their picnic-parties and pleasure
days to a valley as most people would go to the seaside.' There are
high hedges and turf-topped walls, the oak trees are covered in pale
grey lichen and the road from St Merryn becomes a steep dark tunnel
as it approaches St Columb, cut through the rock and arched right
over with trees.

On the windswept Breock Downs to the north-west stand the
'Nine Maidens', the only stone avenue in Cornwall and, close by, one
of the most beautifully sea-blown beech woods in the county. To the
west, looking over the town from 700 feet up, is Castle-an-Dinas, a
great Iron Age hill fort known locally as King Arthur's Castle and
laced with his legends. On the far horizon rises an ever-shifting and
surreal lunar landscape of china clay mountains – the 'Cornish Alps'.

St Columb's fine fifteenth-century church tower commands the
valley: it can be seen and, with its peal of eight bells, heard from afar.
The Celtic St Columba, to whom the great three-aisled church is
dedicated, probably came over from Ireland to preach during the
sixth century and was purportedly pursued upriver by a heathen

tyrant who wanted her to marry his son; she refused, and was martyred at Ruthvoes, two and a half miles away.

Huddled around the churchyard are the older houses of this hillside town, such as the seventeenth-century Glebe House, slate-hung and as Cornish as could be. But although the illustrious Arundell family were lords of the manor from the 1300s until the early 1800s and must have been responsible in part for the building of the present church, the town is predominantly Victorian. Today it retains a fiercely strong character and an atmosphere of great pride. There are lots of individual shops and hardly any chain stores which serve to make one town so like another – only the unforgivably ugly Spar and Co-op shops scar the face of Fore Street.

During the last century St Columb prospered and expanded to become an important Cornish town. The result is glorious. There are narrow streets of slate-hung houses and wonderful 'country grand' Victorian buildings – a classical town hall, a Temperance hall, a bank, Non-Conformist chapels, a large school and, crowning all, the formidable trio of Bank House, Penmellyn House and the Old Rectory by the curious architect William White.

Mr White was employed by the then rector Dr Samuel Walker who, in the late 1840s, was making every effort to groom St Columb for the crown of Cornwall's new cathedral. To a background of *Barchester Towers*-like ecclesiastical whisperings, he was given great encouragement; he even offered his own considerable fortune to further the project. It was then that he asked William White to design the Old Rectory in the hope that it would become the new bishop's palace. White, who had recently set up an office in Truro and was only twenty-four years old, was well qualified for such a job, if mildly eccentric. He was the great-nephew of the naturalist Gilbert White of Selborne, the son of a clergyman, the brother of an arch deacon and the brother-in-law of a bishop. He carried a prayer book and hymnal in his 'Patent Alpine Porte-Knapsack' (his own invention – said to create no pressure on the back or arm) when mountaineering. He disapproved of shaving, sported a beard to his naval and was an advocate of Swedish gymnastics. He was also a brilliant architect. The Old Rectory is romantic, dramatic, uncomplicated and innovative, and is about to become a 'meaderie' – a place where you quaff mead. (The local planning department have a lot to answer for in allowing the most unprepossessing houses to be built along its drive; they fail to make use of either local materials or style.)

The Bank House near the church is also exceptional – rather like a palace on the Piazza in Sienna – and sports some ravishing ironwork, while Penmellyn is more of a homely Cornish manor house.

St Columb never got its cathedral; Truro did in 1877, by which time Dr Walker had died and William White gone off his head. But it got a new school (still used) and a new bank (now Barclays) by the Cornish architect Silvanus Trevail. The game of 'hurling' is still played in St Columb – a distinction it shares only with St Ives. Every Shrove Tuesday for 400 years a small silver ball has been hurled and fought over, rugby fashion, by two teams – townsmen versus countrymen – who run with it either out of the parish or to an appropriate goal a mile or so out of the town. The whole parish forms the playing area, including – just in case you didn't know you were in Cornwall – Tregaswith, Trevonnisck, Tregamere, Talskiddy and Trekenning.

SIDMOUTH

Devon

IF YOU approach Sidmouth on a fine day by the small road from the west and travel through the thick beech woods of Peak Hill, 500 feet above the sea, the first sight of the town below and the slow, arched shoreline between the towering red cliffs takes your breath away. It is the nearest thing to the Italian Riviera we possess. The climate is remarkably mild, as the town lies in a tree-clothed valley whose hills, behind the sea, rise higher than the cliffs. In winter Sidmouth is six degrees warmer than London and it has a lower rainfall than any other South Coast resort.

Until its rarefied resort-life began, Sidmouth was never an important place, although its port at the mouth of the river Sid is grandly called Port Royal. During the seventeenth century the river was 'coaked with chisel and sands by the viscitudes of the tides', but in 1795 Emmanuel Lousada, an enterprising Jewish businessman, saw Sidmouth and decided to convert it into the most elegant and genteel resort in England – a sort of Cheltenham-on-Sea. He bought up a lot of land and set a high standard of fanciful architectural design by building Sidmouth's first *cottage orné*, Peak Hill House, high on a plateau near the cliff's edge. He then began advertising the glories of this sensational spot.

Watering places were by then becoming all the rage, and sea-bathing (preceded by drinking a quart of seawater) was prescribed as being most healthy in mid-winter. Although the first 'water cures' had been prescribed as early as 1660 by Dr Wittie, who had also promoted England's first resort of Scarborough, there were myriad doctors in the eighteenth century who suggested that seawater could cure everything from asthma to deafness. This led to a move towards the sea by the richer classes, ever mindful of their health, and many resorts had doctors for promoters. Once the aristocracy and a member of the royal family had given their seal of approval, the resort took off.

Sidmouth was a perfect success story. Mr Lousada was a brilliant publicist and gradually grand folk from the West Country and even further afield began to build holiday houses on the wooded slopes, a little above and away from the sea, providing the best collection of *cottages ornés* in the country.

Sidmouth's secret is that it has retained its *recherché* atmosphere to this day, when many other Regency resorts, such as Brighton, have not. Its safe distance from London played a part in keeping the Victorian day-trippers at bay, and its dramatic setting prevented a suburban sprawl.

The Grand Duchess Helen of Russia took a house on the esplanade in 1818, and the Duke and Duchess of Kent with their baby daughter, Princess Victoria, took Woolbrook Cottage (now the Royal Glen Hotel) in 1819. In 1820 a cricket field was laid out near the middle of the town. Nowhere could top Sidmouth. The great architect Sir John Soane built Knowle Cottage (which has now been utterly changed) for Lord Despencer, and remarkable *cottages ornés* continued to spring up throughout the last century. This Sidmouth seaside style reached a peak of fancifulness when, in 1856, a Mr Johnstone bought Woodlands Cottage, tastefully Gothicized by Lord Gwydir, and proceeded to adorn it with appendages. He replaced the thatch with hexagonal slates and embellished the dormers with stone icing-sugar barge-boards painted pink, prepared in Italy and shipped to England.

Sidmouth had gone about as far as it could in social and architectural terms. Mr Johnstone's barge-boards were thought to be rather vulgar by the aristocratic corps who still spent their summers under Sidmouth's sky. In the end the call of Nice and Monte Carlo was stronger than the sploshing of waves on the shingle of Jacob's Ladder beach. They left, leaving their wonderful architecture behind them.

Jacob's Ladder beach remains exceptionally beautiful and Connaught Gardens, high on a cliff overlooking it, are some of the best municipal gardens in Britain. Sidmouth's esplanade displays elegant Regency terraces with wrought-iron balconies and the wacky, bow-fronted Gothic Beach House facing out to the sea. (Don't miss the balconies on Fortfield Terrace which is just inland.) Also overlooking the sea but set at slight angles away from its raging storms, are three sumptuous *cottages ornés* built at the end of the eighteenth century – Clifton, Beacon and Rock Cottage. They are in fact as large and dignified as country rectories, and do not fit the appelation as readily as the miniature perfection of Pauntley Cottage. It is still a wonderful town and the walks through its environs in spring are paved with gold – primroses in full flush everywhere.

Sir John Soane Museum

London

FOUR hundred years ago there were fields beside Lincoln's Inn. Members of the legal profession were up in arms when their verdant open spaces were threatened by a developer called William Newton, who wanted to build thirty-two houses. He won the day in the late 1630s, and so the engulfing of the fields began. More development followed, but today we look upon this handsome City square of Lincoln's Inn Fields, packed with lawyers' offices, as a peaceful escape from the river of traffic in Holborn. An air of strict legality hovers above the plane trees in the central gardens. The houses are reserved – until, that is, you notice the south-facing No. 13, which breaks all the rules: flooded with sun whenever there is any and easily my favourite house in London. It belonged to Sir John Soane, the architect of the Bank of England and the Dulwich Art Gallery, and he left it to the nation. The strange façade was originally designed by Soane as a loggia, which he later filled in with windows to give extra space in the house. It would never get planning permission today!

Soane was a genius. His architecture was wild and annoyed the purists. He was miles ahead of his time, combining a slow-arched elegance with amazingly modern details such as recycling the wasted heat from chimneys through the passages of a house. The son of an Essex bricklayer, he was born in Goring-on-Thames and started his life as an errand boy. He entered the office of the architect George Dance the Younger and later of Henry Holland. His talent at drawing was soon recognized. He won the Royal Academy Gold Medal for a design of a triumphal bridge. Sir William Chambers saw it and introduced him to George III and his career began to soar. His house in Lincoln's Inn Fields, which he combined as a home, a studio and a gallery, encapsulates his brilliance.

The Sir John Soane Museum, as his house is now called, could easily have been wrecked by some whizz-kid with progressive and popularizing ideas. Instead it has been very gently restored and enlivened by its latest curator, Peter Thornton. There could be no more pleasurable way to spend a lunch hour then to linger here, and if anyone is about to design or decorate a house they should not embark without first visiting this house. It contains more ingenious ideas than I have had hot breakfasts, and certainly many more than you will ever glean from magazines.

Soane first moved to 12 Lincoln's Inn Fields in 1792 and, over the next forty-five years, added Nos 13 and 14 and filled them to the brim, incorporating every architectural trick he knew. As soon as you venture through the front door you lose all sense of orientation. Nothing is normal. The use of space is quite extraordinary. The dining room, which is combined with the library, has mirrored arches and shutters and circles above the books. The reflections are endless, and by candlelight dazzling. Even on a dull day the fire irons and fenders, the furniture and worn leather seats glisten with their weekly polishings. It's a man's room, painted Pompeian red and bronzed green, as is the little study and dressing room directly off it. It is like a ship's cabin and not an inch is wasted.

The breakfast room is probably my favourite room in the house, with its domed ceiling and inset mirrors which give it a sparkling brilliance; but it is so satisfactorily practical as well. The picture room, where you can see Hogarth's *The Rake's Progress*, has huge and surprising swinging doors housing more pictures than you would think possible in so small a space.

There are optically elusive corridors of Corinthian columns and crypts beneath which were once the back yards of the houses. The custodians refer to them as the 'Valley of death' since they contain so many remnants of Greek tombs and a gigantic Egyptian sarcophagus. Although Soane was purported to be a depressive the upstairs drawing rooms could not be merrier. They are painted in the most wonderful 'patent' yellow with stiff silk curtains to match, and when the sun shines through the stained glass on the sides of the glazed-in loggia you might easily be in the South of France.

Soane was an obsessive collector. He scanned every sales catalogue and haunted the salesrooms. He did not always go to the auctions, but Mrs Soane, a considerable heiress, often did and it was she who bid for *The Rake's Progress* at Christie's in 1802 and secured the eight canvasses for £570. The house is stuffed with *objets d'art*, architectural models, drawings and paintings (including Turners), all arranged in an inimitable and intimate way. It is not *at all* like a museum – just a wonderful private house belonging to an extraordinary man.

SOUTHEASE

Sussex

The great hills of the South Country
    They stand along the sea:
And it's there walking in the high woods
    That I could wish to be,
And the men that were boys when I was a boy
    Walking along with me.

IF YOU walk up on to those great rounded hills, as Hilaire Belloc did, between Eastbourne and Brighton, where beech woods are sliced sideways by the wind and from whose heights you can sometimes see the sea, you will feel better than you did before.

Resembling a long chain of huge soft pillows dented with curving combes, the South Downs are an archipelago of separate islands divided by rivers which run from the north down to the sea and thwart their drift and flow. The Lavant, the Arun, the Adur, the Ouse and the Cuckmere cut through the chalk mass and create wide and gentle valleys between. These downs are different in character from those of Wiltshire, Berkshire and Dorset.

Sussex is a kingdom of its own, Saxon through and through and as different from Celtic Cornwall as chalk from cheese. In the whole county there is only one Celtic place name: the camp near Lewes, Caer Bryn – or Mount Caburn, as it is now called. It was once islanded by the Ouse and the Glynde, and was thus a veritable stronghold. If you stand high on the hill looking north-eastwards from the quiet, uneventful village of Southease, you can see the outline of Mount Caburn.

Travelling through this red-brick, tile-hung, clap-boarded, flint and thatched country, past the modest village of Rodmell – which has a wonderful petrol station run by the blacksmith Frank Dean, whose smithy is hard by – you'll find a dead-end sign to Southease turning you down into the Ouse valley. Twenty-seven people live here in a scattering of houses and cottages centred around a triangular green. At Christmas there is a candlelit carol service in the small flint-and-rubble church, which has a simple, barn-like interior and a beautiful organ. (In the church in the village where I used to live, we weren't allowed to light candles because of the 'fire hazard'.)

The strange, round tower of the church is one of only three in Sussex, all of them near by. One is at the top of Lewes High Street and the other at the neighbouring village of Piddinghoe. Perhaps a builder from East Anglia settled here in the Ouse valley in the twelfth century and built the towers he remembered from back home. Below the church there is an ancient thatched cottage and, along the bottom side of the green, a wall of unknapped flint surrounds a wealden-type house. A sign says 'Unsuitable for Motors' and the road leads to the bottom of the valley.

Before the river Ouse was channelled into a deep-cut canal and its low-tide mud flats crossed with dykes a spring tide would have come up to the village green. It is hard to believe that Southease was once a thriving fishing village, depending on large hauls of herrings and smaller ones of porpoises for its livelihood. Today there are straggling flint farm buildings with orangey-red tiled roofs sweeping low where boats once moored, and Guernsey cows come home across the meadows as though things had never been different.

The road leads on between rustling reeds as tall as an elephant's eye to a hump-backed bridge across the straightened river. From the banks you can catch sea trout or, once a year, watch the raft race between Newhaven and Lewes. It is hard not to imagine the ghost of Virginia Woolf floating downstream towards the sea three miles on. She drowned herself from these banks over fifty years ago, and her sad husband Leonard continued to live in their old farmhouse at Rodmell until his death in 1962.

The Bloomsbury set have lived in and loved and hymned and painted these downs for their special light and their timeless quality.

Kipling, too, celebrated the region in his poem, 'The Run of the Downs':

> The Weald is good, the Downs are best –
> I'll give you the run of 'em, East to West . . .
> The Downs are sheep, the Weald is corn,
> You be glad you are Sussex born!

The South Downs aren't only good for sheep and artists, they are also perfect for training racehorses. The legendary Ryan Price trained here, and champions John Dunlop and Guy Harwood would be nowhere else. Up at the back of Southease, towards Peacehaven and Rottingdean, where the downs are at their biggest and best and Brakey Bottom winds its giant combe like a river, between the hills there is the pretty flint-and-brick village of Telscombe where Shannon Lass was trained on the Telscombe Tye gallop. She won the Grand National in 1902.

SOUTHEND-ON-SEA

Essex

WHEN I rang up Fenchurch Street Station enquiries to find out about trains to Southend-on-Sea, I reached an extraordinarily enthusiastic transport buff, to whom I talked for ten minutes about all the stations on the line. Although it turned out that he lived in Margate, he couldn't recommend the trip to Southend too highly. There are regular trains from Fenchurch Street and they take forty minutes, which is about as long as you have to wait for your food in some City restaurants. You pass through East End-ing Limehouse, Barking and Upminster and then strike out into low, lost, unsung Thames-side Essex. From West Horndon, Laindon and Basildon, the train speeds on to muddier and marshier Pitsea and Benfleet. To the south you can survey the eerie Island of Canvey, reclaimed from the great Thames estuary in the seventeenth century at the same time as the East Anglian Fens, by the Dutchman Cornelius Vermuyden. A few Dutch labourers settled here at the time and built themselves cottages, two of which survive – both octagonal. Most of the island, which is now spread with bungalows and chalets, lies below high-tide level and there is a massive new concrete sea-wall with gaps which can be closed by floodgates to defend it. It had not yet been built in 1953 when, on the night of 31 January a storm swept over the island and fifty-eight people were drowned.

At Leigh-on-Sea, which is the next station on the line, there are cockle, mussel, whelk and jellied eel stalls on the mud flats between the train and the estuary. High above the old fishing village, with its Crooked Billet Inn and its High Street leading down to the shore, stands the church of St Clement. All is surrounded by nineteenth-century development in what is today a suburb of Southend, as are the next two stops at Chalkwell and Westcliff.

When you get out at Southend Station and start the short walk down the bustling High Street towards the water and see the longest pier in the world venturing out into the Channel, you cannot help but feel you are on holiday – even if it's just your lunch hour. The change from the City's serious atmosphere to the frivolous gaiety of Southend is total. Whatever the weather – and I usually come here in the winter months – the seafront is dedicated to pure pleasure. It is also beautiful.

You would never guess that gregarious Southend has its roots in a twelfth-century priory in what was one of Essex's oldest villages, Prittlewell. From Priory Crescent, a path leads across Priory Park to the Clunic remains of church, cloisters, refectory and living quarters. A thriving community of oyster fishermen had grown up around the priory at its southern end – hence the name Southend. After the Dissolution of the Monasteries, some of the buildings were converted into a house and the church was pulled down. Over the succeeding centuries the house was added to and given a Georgian façade and, after the First World War, was presented to the Corporation of Southend. It is now the Borough Museum.

The first attempts to transform the place into a holiday resort began at the end of the eighteenth century. Entrepreneurial developers, cashing in on people's hypochondriacal fixation with their health, were alighting on likely sites all around England's coast, but Southend was slow to catch on compared to Margate and Brighton. Princess Caroline of Wales and her daughter Charlotte both stayed here at the very beginning of the nineteenth century and the new resort became briefly fashionable – Regency terraces were built up on the esplanade above the sea as well as a grand stucco hotel which gained the title of 'Royal' after the princess's visit. However, by the 1820s the aristocracy had already deserted Southend and, although it retained a quieter, posher end around Thorpe Bay (still the smart place to live), it was the coming of the railway in the 1850s and the creation of Bank Holidays in 1870 that brought a different kind of success – hordes of day-trippers from London.

Southend's clamorous-cockle-stall reputation began: London's East End could be by the seaside in under an hour. The hub of the resort, Marine Parade, gradually filled up with public houses; slot machines, amusement arcades, bingo halls, playgrounds and funfairs abounded and the town spread ever outwards to Shoebury Ness and Benfleet around over a thousand acres of parks.

Despite its present size, Southend is still elegant and still exciting. The pier stretches for nearly a mile and a half. In 1939 the Royal Navy took it over and renamed it HMS *Leigh*. It became an operations centre and assembly point from which nearly 3,500 convoys sailed. A railway running along the promenade deck the length of the pier carried the sick and wounded in one direction and supplies in the other. Today you can still take the train to the end of the pier and sit, halfway to France, watching gigantic ships sail by.

TEESDALE

County Durham

HIGH FORCE could be in South America. Standing below its foaming, boiling mass which falls with a roar from the 70-foot-high sill into the deep dark pool of burnt umber-coloured river, you expect Jeremy Irons dressed as a missionary to appear from behind a rock. Instead you meet the occasional professional back-packing rambler in lightweight rainwear which makes a feeble swishing sound compared to the thunder of this wonderful waterfall. The newly made path which winds down from the road, lost many of the 100-foot-high trees which shaded it in the devastating hurricane of 1992, but there are moss-covered crags with stalwart beeches clinging to them by octopus-like roots and ash saplings sticking to vertical cliffs above the great river Tees.

This is not South America but County Durham, the land of prince bishops and always a different domain, a county palatine set apart from England and Scotland. The mighty river Tyne marks its northern boundary and the fair Tees spreads its pools and tumbles through the south. At Scotch Corner, where the A1 strikes onwards dragging its hurried victims in steady streams, you can turn off westwards and make for Greta Bridge, one of the most graceful in all England. It spans the river Greta in a simple sweep and was designed in the eighteenth century by John Carr of York for the owners of the house and wooded park of Rokeby; its Grecian entrance gates stand beside the bridge. Just beyond is the Morrit Arms, a coaching inn which has long been my favourite stopping place. Dickens stayed here while researching *Nicholas Nickleby* and the bar is covered in murals painted in 1946 by Gilroy, the originator of the Guinness advertisements.

Rokeby's park is sliced through by the A66 dual carriageway but, once crossed, the journey up the valley of the Tees to High Force begins, past the glorious yellow ochre-coloured house of Rokeby, its plain Palladian façade looking straight into the morning sun, reserved and elegant. Velázquez's *Rokeby Venus* (who was said by Augustus John to have the most slappable bottom in the National Gallery) once hung here, bought by J. B. S. Morrit in 1813. He wrote to his close friend Sir Walter Scott about the hanging of 'my fine picture of Venus's backside', which he had placed in a suitably high position so that 'the ladies may avert their downcast eyes without difficulty and connoisseurs steal a glance'.

On up the valley the spectacular ruins of Egglestone Abbey stand on a plateau high over a steep, deep gorge above the Tees – a few cottages edge the small sheep-grazed green beside it – but the image of this quiet idyll is soon hit for six as the road leads on by the sight of the mountainous Bowes Museum, a gigantic French château, plucked from the Loire and dropped by the Tees in the nineteenth century. It looks positively startling and houses the most wonderfully eclectic collection of art and artefacts, all thanks to George Bowes, the bastard son of the Earl of Strathmore. It stands on the edge of Barnard Castle, one of the best market towns in England with wide streets of handsome houses – some of the local pinkish-grey stone, some white stuccoed with black-painted window surrounds. A beautiful octagonal market cross commands the view down the steep hill called The Bank and the great Norman ruined castle rises up dramatically above the river.

Out from the town the road leads on up verdant Teesdale, which secretes its treasures of spring gentians, bird's-eye primroses, cinquefoils, nine species of lady's mantle and, in the high pastures, 'double-dumpling' orchids. On past walled and tree-speckled pastures, through Lartington and ravishing, wide-greened villages like Cotherstone and Romaldkirk – the latter almost ridiculously pretty. Mickleton, in bigger, bolder country, is set sliding down the side of a hill among sycamores, and along the road the lost railway is choked with rosebay willowherb. The steepest fields are thick with ragwort.

There are farms on the hillsides all around and a cattle market smelling of disinfectant beside the bridge which leads over to Middleton-in-Teesdale, a fine and satisfactory little town with some proper shops – general stores selling shrimping nets and potatoes, a family baker, butcher and chemist, a fishing tackle shop and an unforgivably ugly Co-op with red shiny plastic facings. There are big beech and sycamore trees down the main street, Horse Market, a huge pinnacled Methodist chapel and the grandest of arches leading to nowhere but a few cottages and fields.

Leaving Middleton, the capital of Upper Teesdale, the country becomes bleaker with outcrops of the dark resistant Whinstone rock which forms vertical cliffs, scars and waterfalls. Cauldron Snout, the most spectacular cascade, is hidden in the hills, and near Low Force Europe's earliest suspension bridge spans the Tees, but it is High Force, the largest and mightiest waterfall in England, which caps all.

THORNEY IN THE FENS

Cambridgeshire

Few go to the Fens for their holidays. Some people are actually frightened of them and perhaps, helped by the ghost stories of M. R. James, imagine being stranded somewhere near March on a stormy November night. No bus-loads of tourists travel the roads, as straight as a die beside deep, dark dykes and 'roddons', or wonder at the huge, broad sunsets or the eerie and isolated farms amid vast expanses of finely worked, rich, black soil. 'The arch of heaven spreads about the Fens,' wrote Charles Kingsley, 'more ample than elsewhere, as over the open sea, and that vastness gave and still gives, such cloud-banks, such sunrises, as can be seen nowhere else in these isles.' This the 'Land of Three Quarter Sky', is a place of hard toil, where people have always had to struggle against wind and flood – every front garden is as neat as a pin and its fiercely independent people are said to keep their money under their beds. The Fen country has long been a kingdom of its own and in some ways it has stronger ties with Holland and Denmark than with England: it was a Dutch engineer, Cornelius Vermuyden, who oversaw the draining of the Fens in the seventeenth century.

Long before Vermuyden came to this watery, windswept country, the only habitable places (after the Romans had left and their efficient drainage system had fallen into disuse) were the scattered archipelago of islands on the barely visible rises above sea-level. They were perfect places for early monastic settlements, for the fish and fowl were plentiful and the solitude total. Abbeys and priories sprang up at Swavesey, Swaffham Bulbeck, Chatteris, Spinney, Fordham, Denny, Upwell, Anglesey and Soham, but the most celebrated were Ely and Thorney. Ely Cathedral remains the great mother-ship of the Fens, with her sails set so high into the wide East Anglian sky that you can see them from miles and miles away in all directions. Thorney, on the other hand, did not survive intact, but is a lovely and little-visited place which you might have whizzed by on your way from wonderful Wisbech to Peterborough. But I'll bet you didn't stop.

If you do stop, this is what you'll find: one of the finest and most exemplary nineteenth-century model villages in England with a strange, high water-tower as its pivot and, on the other side of the main road, a beautiful abbey-church almost a thousand years old. Beside it are some pretty seventeenth-century houses, a small green and a winding street leading away and out into fenland. Thorney is not like other Fen villages and towns – it has more trees and has experienced an almost continual succession of benevolent landlords and good husbandry for nearly 1,500 years.

Thorney means 'Isle of Thorns', but when a group of Celtic monks settled here in the seventh century it was called Arncairg, 'Isle of the Anchorites'. They built an abbey and farmed land once full of brambles. Then in 870 the Danes razed everything to the ground. The famous Bishop Ethelwold began to re-found a Benedictine abbey a hundred years later, a small, much-altered piece of which remains today. Along with countless other religious institutions, the Mitred Abbey of Thorney was dissolved in 1529 and its buildings, as expansive as those at Ely, began to decay. One hundred and forty-six tons of the abbey stone were shipped to Cambridge to build Corpus Christi College Chapel; most was dispersed among local churches and villages.

Many other fenland abbeys and priories fell into ruin, but Thorney found a guardian angel in the form of Sir William Russell, who bought the whole village, lock, stock and barrel, together with 6,500 acres in 1550. Sir William's descendants, later the dukes of Bedford, went on to own Thorney for an unbroken 362 years. They built a *pied-à-terre* opposite the church, whose entrance, between two of the grandest rusticated gateposts you ever saw, is irresistible. In 1660 the Bedfords added to the little Elizabethan house a ravishing four-square Restoration house with a delicately hipped roof and deep-coved cornice under the eaves. Beside it is a large walled garden. Subsequent members of the House of Russell showed a great affection for Thorney and were frequent visitors and good landlords.

The Victorian Duke of Bedford, following in the wake of other fabulously rich and philanthropic industrialists and agriculturalists of the time, decided to make Thorney into the ultimate model village. He was shocked by the suppression of the working classes in agricultural communities and believed that if people were happy with their circumstances they would work better. His magnanimity paid off: G. M. Young referred to Thorney in *Victorian England* as 'the most successful experiment in social organization that England had so far seen'. The duke built rows of neo-Jacobean terraced cottages for his workers in the local pale, watery-yellow brick, with clustered chimneys and leaded lights, and also some particularly pretty square double cottages with Dutch gables disguising their lean-tos. By the 1880s Thorney had its own railway station and gasworks (all the cottages were gas-lit), its own school, reading room and water-tower. It remains a model to this day.

THRUMPTON HALL

Nottinghamshire

UNNOTICED Nottinghamshire, through which the M1 and the Midland Railway speed, would be unlikely to feature in a list of the top ten counties of England. Though it may be revered by cricketers and loyally loved by its inhabitants, it is generally unappreciated and unconsidered by travellers in search of the picturesque. Apart from the romantic escapades of Robin Hood in Sherwood Forest, even its past is dim: for long centuries Nottinghamshire was by-passed and, according to county history, completely 'undistinguished by dramatic episodes'. Only the last two centuries have brought dramatic changes. Industry sprang up in the countryside in an altogether haphazard fashion. Factories and pit heads, power stations and pylons have sprouted amidst farms and villages, mild manors and ducal estates.

In *Nottingham and the Mining Country*, Nottinghamshire's famous son, D. H. Lawrence, accused the Victorian promoters of industry of condemning workers to ' . . . ugliness, ugliness, ugliness: meaningless and formless and ugly surroundings, ugly ideas, ugly religion, ugly hope, ugly love, ugly furniture, ugly houses . . . The human soul needs actual beauty even more than bread.'

But there is beauty here in grim, stalwart, unselfconscious Nottinghamshire. It is here, off the M1, somewhere between the endless brown signs to Alton Towers and Donnington racing circuit. Elder flower and hogweed bloom in the hedgerows. There are eight giant, smoke-belching cooling towers around a central chimney as tall as the Eiffel Tower, alongside a huge mountain of coal. Near by is an eighteenth-century raggle-taggle ruby-red-brick farmstead, bursting with cattle and geese. The sky behind is laced with rows of pylons. This is Ratcliffe-on-Soar. Just beyond is the turn to Thrumpton.

Over the hill and down through an ash copse towards a dead end lies the small village. The poplars and limes show the backs of their leaves before the rain. On either side of the lane are the odd sixties houses, well settled into 'low maintenance' shrub gardens. Here at the lane's bend is the original village and the church of All Saints, with a squat fourteenth-century tower; the chancel was rebuilt by the architect George Street in the 1870s. Beside the entrance is a moving monument of a recumbent soldier in uniform under a canopy, built in memory of three young villagers lost in the First World War. The church is particularly elaborate inside, with a fine monument to Gervase Pigot, who died in 1669, which he swankingly commissioned for himself. During his lifetime he had also glorified the great house of Thrumpton Hall, just down the village street, which his father, also named Gervase, had built at the beginning of the seventeenth century.

The estate had been confiscated in 1605 from the Powdrills who, together with the Babbingtons at Ratcliffe-on-Soar, were the principal local families involved in the Gunpowder Plot.

The present H-shaped Jacobean hall of sumptuous red brick was given its swooping Dutch gables by Gervase Pigot II. There are loggias on either side, one giving on to a lake formed by a quiet backwater of the river Trent. The park is ravishing and sports a cricket pitch. The estate passed on to John Emerton, who improved the village in the eighteenth century by building pretty cottages along the street. It then passed down the female line to Lord Byron, the poet's cousin, who built still more picturesque cottages and turreted brick entrance arches to the hall in true Isfahan style. Thrumpton Hall's secret world, hidden by a small ridge from the power station, is unexpected and overwhelming.

Winding on down the lane past low meadows full of buttercups and an Arab horse or two, you reach the banks of the mighty Trent – a sweeping river of currents, weirs, locks and floodbanks. A caravan or two lurk among the Friesian cows and under the great ash and willow trees, while on the near horizon is Nottingham, 'Queen of the Midlands', another world again.

THE TUNNEL HOUSE INN

Coates, Wiltshire

Near the little-visited source of Thames, secreted between the limestone villages of Coates and Tarlton, is the most spectacular and unexpected surprise. Little do you know what you are in for as you wind between dry-stone walls and clipped hedges in that transitional countryside stranded between the flat fields of north Wiltshire and the deep, dark, wooded valleys towards Bisley.

Near the railway are the workings of a lost canal. Then a strange circular lengthsman's cottage appears above the brambles (a 'lengthsman' was responsible for the upkeep of a certain stretch of road, railway or canal). Nearby you see the sign to the Tunnel House Inn. You take an unmetalled track, hanging high above a steep canal cutting, arched over and dramatized by great beeches and ending at the inn. Below you, down a stepped and slippery bank, the canal enters the most exciting tunnel in England – at the time it was built, in the late eighteenth century, it was the biggest engineering achievement in the world.

The Thames and Severn Canal was never a great commercial success. It was designed to link the two great rivers so that cheaper coal from the Shropshire collieries could reach the ever-mushrooming city of London. Soon after it was inaugurated, the Oxford Canal opened and took a lot of its trade, and when the railway finally came in 1840 the Thames and Severn began its slow and inevitable decline. It was abandoned in 1927 and left to nature.

This eastern portal to the tunnel, however, with its huge blocks of rusticated stone, its columns and pediment, became a haunt for pilgrims in search of the Romantic. The niches, originally intended for statues of Father Thames and Madam Sabrina, became smothered in ivy; fallen beech trees lay spreadeagled across the cutting; and the tunnel's entrance, choked with black mud, looked like the gate to Hades. My father brought me here as a small child and the romance of the place has never diminished for me.

The abandoned canal tunnel was not the only reason he came here. The inn was a veritable haven on a lonely road and he never said no to a nip of whisky. In the early fifties, before the house was damaged by fire, it was three storeys high, having been built in the 1780s to house some of the numerous tunnel workers. Today it still feels instantly welcoming.

Along the bar and around the two log fires is the most eclectic mix of objects and people imaginable: hearty, fresh-faced Cirencester students; arty bearded craftsmen accompanied by women in felt hats with babies on their hips; horsy girls in puffas and jods with Jilly Cooper (she lives near) giggles; local farm workers with tractor oil up to their arm pits; and nattily suited estate agents from Tetbury. You cannot but fit in amongst the piles of old copies of *Hello!*, stuffed weasels and otters, mad sofas, redundant dentists' chairs, copper pans, old advertising signs, carnations in cut-glass vases, juke box and fruit machines (soundless, on their lowest volume at lunch time anyway), good stew, postcards of pert gigantic breasts on sunny beaches and photographs of racehorses winning at Cheltenham. The owner Chris Kite races dogs at Swindon and his son is the head lad for the trainer Jenny Pitman.

I doubt the tap room was ever so jolly 200 years before: cutting a 3,817-yard (2.2-mile) tunnel through the Cotswold escarpment was a hard way of making a living. Though the numbers killed in the process were never recorded, the local graveyards grew considerably at the time. The men were mostly miners from Derbyshire, Somerset and Cornwall and the engineers in overall charge were Josiah Clowes and Robert Whitworth. The initial contractor employed by the canal company, Charles 'Feckless' Jones, agreed a price of seven guineas a yard for a 15-foot-diameter bore and he pledged to finish the tunnel in four years. Several contractors later, it was finished in five. In April 1789 the first shipments of coal were 'legged' through (men lay on

The almshouses,
Lyford.

Mapperton's eastern
face and Elizabethan
garden house.

Maud Heath's column
above East Tytherton.

Left: Iford Manor gardens.

Top right: Chapel of St Michael, Rame Head.

Bottom right: Restormel Castle.

Below: Prideaux Place.

Above: Church of St Columba, St Columb Major.

Above: The breakfast room, Sir John Soane Museum.

Below: Cottage *orné* at Sidmouth.

Southease.

The pier at Southend.

The river Tees from
Barnard Castle.

Top left: Thorney in the Fens.

Top right: The Thames and Severn Canal tunnel entrance near Coates.

Left: Loggia at Thrumpton Hall.

Above: Church of St Bartholomew, Warleggan.

Below: The Watts Chapel, Compton.

Below: Weymouth.

Above: Church of St Andrew, Winterbourne Tomson.

Above: Wistman's Wood.

Above: York Station.

top of the barge roof and walked along the tunnel's ceiling) from the western end at the idyllic village of Sapperton – bastion of the Arts and Crafts movement at the turn of the century. Sapperton's portal, though castellated, is less grand and built of brick.

Over the last few years the Cotswold Canals Trust has cleared the long cutting with its cathedral nave of beeches and on Sundays it runs trips in a silent, flat-bottomed boat a third of the way down the tunnel. It is an eerie and magical experience, gliding in the ice-blue, crystal-clear water on and on into the darkness, through the hollowed-out golden limestone, until the light at the end of the tunnel becomes a pin-prick. In its middle section the canal becomes unnavigable. The bed of fuller's earth through which it passes caused subsidence problems from the outset. Anyway, by this time, as the odd drip of water from the palest pink stalactite hits your neck, you are quite pleased to be heading back again.

WARLEGGAN

Cornwall

BODMIN MOOR is a hundred square miles of wild, desolate and beautiful country dominated by two mountains, Rough Tor and Brown Willy, where the dark pools, lost tin mines, fly-eating sundew plants and strange standing stones are hard to find unless you know the area.

In the 1890s the young rector of Warleggan, the Reverend Charles Ernest Lambert, used to walk across the moor with his terrier every Sunday from Warleggan to Temple, where he took a service in the early afternoon. He would then be back in time for evensong at Warleggan. One Sunday he never returned. He seemed in good health, according to a local farmer, William Mitchell, who used to tease the Rector for being fat; 'It isn't fat, it's muscle; I never felt better in my life.' He was found dead on the moor the following Wednesday with his dog beside him.

Through the churchless village of Mount with its beautiful whitewashed post office (where the youngest postmistress in Britain, fifteen-year-old Barbara Webster, once served), the Methodist chapel and ever uglier peddledashed bungalows spreading outwards, the road narrows and dips down steeply. It passes past high banks of nut and hawthorn, ferns, spent foxgloves, blue vetch and hogweed until you reach a bridge over the tumbling Warleggan river which rushes peaty brown from the moor in a series of waterfalls over huge boulders. All around are tall beech trees, their trunks covered in moss. On upwards and into the light again past a slate-hung Georgian farm and eventually you will get to Warleggan – or Warth-la-gan, which means 'the higher place on the downs'. The tiny village hangs on the side of this steep hillside, looking away from the moor and out over a patchwork of hedged and walled fields across the valley.

There is a small Methodist chapel, a former school, now Badger's Cottage, a Victorian letter box and, lying on the bank, a great round granite stone for banding wheels. Tucked into the hillside is a row of three tiny moorstone cottages. Through their white front gates, slate-paved paths lead through lush little gardens of box, laurel and hydrangea to the front doors. The garden walls are sprinkled with patches of lichen and small ferns, and just below the last gate is the redundant village pump, soon to be restored.

The fifteenth-century church of silvery, well-weathered granite is glorious and lies safely tucked into the ground as though anchored against the blasts from the moor. On Saturday 14 March 1818, however, a thundercloud burst over the church and the tower was shivered to pieces by lightning. Fragments fell on the church roof and destroyed much of the interior, narrowly missing the clerk, who was just leaving after his preparations for the Sunday service. The inside is hence mostly Victorian restoration, but the outside is worth a long journey. To the east of the churchyard, if you look through the gateway you will see a beautiful Gothic-windowed barn half smothered in ivy. To the west, in the deep shade of huge beech trees is a wooden door in the former rectory garden wall.

The plain Regency Warleggan rectory is now called The Rookery and was sold by the church commissioners in the 1950s the very day after eighty-three-year-old Reverend Frederick William Densham was found dead on the stairs. Cyril Keast, a Methodist who still lives in the village and had a great respect for the rector, said, 'The Saturday he was found dead I was disgusted to see him carried away by the police in an open pick-up truck just covered with a blanket with his feet showing out the back.' It was a sad end to a kind, intelligent and misunderstood man whose memory has been maligned. Daphne du Maurier, in her *Vanishing Cornwall*, tried to read something sinister into his eccentricity and fabricated the story that he still haunts the place. She never met him.

He came to Warleggan in 1933, having been on a sabbatical in Ceylon. He was a highly cultivated man and would visit the

Methodist chapel services and ask their preachers to preach in his own church. In his open-minded approach he was fifty years ahead of his time, but this upset his parishioners and no one went to church. For twenty years he conducted services each Sunday and preached long sermons to no one save a few cardboard cut-out figures and the odd outsider, such as my parents and my brother and I when we were on holiday in Cornwall. Afterwards we would go through the door in the wall to the lovely playground he had constructed, which included a pond for toy boats, swings and slides, a pony-trap wheel on its axle, and a sand pit. Around the darkly rhododendroned garden he had created arbours with seats and tables where he placed writing sets in waterproof tins. Encircling the whole demesne was an 8-foot-high wire fence. The Reverend Densham was terrified of being burgled and kept Alsatian dogs to guard him. He bought buckets and porridge and oats in bulk, kept several beds made up in case evacuees from the war arrived, and talked about theology to my parents while my brother and I played. His hermit-like existence made him a legend.

THE WATTS GALLERY AND CHAPEL

Compton, Surrey

Tucked under the high chalk ridge of the Hog's Back, where you can see miles of wooded country stretching into the blue distance on either side, is a pocket of Surrey worth travelling hours to find. Beyond the relentless roundabouts, lurching you this way and that, on the outskirts of the village of Compton is one of the most curious religious buildings in England.

It stands on a little hill, this Byzantine-looking basilica of bright red brick, among cherry blossom and dark fingers of black Irish yew looking for all the world like cypresses – a piece of Tuscany in the Home Counties. The steep path lined with flowers zigzags up towards the Watts Mortuary Chapel, built at the turn of the century by Mary Watts, with no professional assistance beyond that of the local builder and blacksmith, and a team of villagers trained in the pottery she had founded.

'I always hoped it would *tone down*,' she said, but it never did. The chapel is built on a circular and cruciform plan, part of Mary Watts's carefully calculated symbolism – the circle of eternity with the cross of faith running through it. You walk in the Norman-arched doorway covered with terracotta heads of angels, each worked by villagers, some looking downwards in sympathy, some upward in hope. But this austere exterior gives no inkling of what is to come. Inside is the richest, rarest display of Art Nouveau you have ever seen in your life. A glistening green, scarlet, gold and silver mass of seraphs, angels and trees of life, their roots and tendrils winding wildly this way and that, smother the high, domed interior. Mary Watts called it her 'glorified wallpaper'; my seventeen-year-old son David called it 'seriously wicked'. The whole surface is in fact moulded and incised in gesso, which is a sort of cross between *papier-*

mâché and plastic. I first saw it when I was ten and never forgot its brilliance, nor my astonishment.

Up behind the chapel is a long cloister facing out across the valley; in front is the grave of the sculptor G. F. Watts, to whose memory the chapel is dedicated. Wilfred Blunt called him 'England's Michelangelo'. His painting *Hope* and his statue *Physical Energy* are certainly up the same street. The original plaster model for the latter, probably the largest piece of sculpture undertaken with no patron or commission, is here in Compton. So is his model for Tennyson, the bronze of which stands in the city of Lincoln – a glorious 12-foot-high likeness of the gloomy-looking Lincolnshire poet with his huge wolfhound. The models are in the sculpture gallery of the Watts Museum, a little up the road from the chapel and as wonderfully informal a place as one could wish to visit.

The gallery was built in 1903, a mixture of Surrey cottage style and Scottish Art Nouveau, of red-tiled gables and pebbledash, of wafer-brick sunburst keystones and green glazed pottery. A fig tree grows around a terracotta bust by Watts in a little sunken garden of box hedges, rosemary and Compton ware pots. Inside are well over a hundred of Watts's paintings, including the self-portait painted at the age of seventeen and *The Wounded Heron*, which was exhibited at the Royal Academy three years later. Watts had a frail constitution – he was often ill and depressed – but was lionized by female patrons, who protected him from the drudgery of everyday life. Lady Holland first nurtured his talent and in 1851 he became the permanent guest of Mr and Mrs Thoby Prinsep at Holland House in London. 'He came to stay for three days and stayed thirty years,' said Mrs Prinsep, who in the end persuaded him to marry Ellen Terry when he was forty-seven and she sixteen. It was a disastrous idea and they soon parted. When he was sixty-nine he married Mary Fraser Tytler, thirty years his junior, who was also an artist and lived at Compton, and they lived happily ever after. Watts was twice offered a baronetcy by Gladstone but he refused.

Being in the Wattses world is an unforgettable experience because their presence is so strong, but do not miss the more normal pleasures of the village of Compton. Here is cosy Surrey at its best – quaint, genuine black-and-white or brick cottages with steep tiled roofs, leaded panes and tall chimneys, with neat little gardens before them and a church of overwhelming beauty and simplicity: bright white chalkstone inside, with bold Norman columns and arches and a unique double sanctuary – the first-floor altar has a Norman rail of arched oak. It is as utterly different from the Watts Mortuary Chapel as chalk is from cheese. DO NOT MISS EITHER.

WEYMOUTH

Dorset

A FRIEND of mine once described returning to England after a long time away in Africa. He travelled slowly across Europe and caught the ferry from Cherbourg to Weymouth. 'I had this dread about seeing England again,' he explained. 'When you arrive at Dover or Heathrow after an absence it can look so dreary and depressing. Weymouth is by far the best approach. You see it first like a Regency print in the distance and as you get nearer there are small sailing boats and you can just discern people walking along the esplanade. Everything is on a human scale. It's perfect England.'

There is no doubt that it is better to approach Weymouth by sea than by the road, for its outskirts are half wrecked. Not the reedy Radipole Lake – where swans glide and hundreds of small boats are packed into rows like cars in a car park waiting to head downstream for the sea – but where the roundabouts are littered with signs and the brick of the new DIY centre is a relentless and unforgivable scarlet.

But once you get into the heart of Weymouth, its seaside glory all around, you wonder why on earth you haven't been here more often. No wonder it is called the English Naples. It is as pretty as anything you could wish for with its huge, graceful and almost imperceptibly curving bay of fine pale sand. It faces east and is protected by the breezy heights of the Purbeck Hills. Beside the sea, bow fronts and bow windows abound and there are canopied seats which look like white wedding cakes, laced with nineteenth-century ironwork, there are no 'important' buildings like the Pavilion Royal in Brighton, just good English eighteenth- and nineteenth-century seaside terraces and hotels which all mix and look well together – Portland stone, Georgian and Regency stucco alongside Victorian red brick. There is a particularly jolly polychrome brick hotel called the Royal Hotel with pepper-pots topped by fishscale-tiled roofs.

The old harbour is full of stuccoed, bow-windowed houses painted different colours, small inns and ship's chandlers with winding streets behind. Weymouth was an important port even before the Romans came to Maiden Castle, and for centuries played a star role in stirring periods of maritime history. The town provided twenty ships for the Siege of Calais (only two less than Bristol and the Port of London) and six for Drake's fleet in the Spanish Armada, and has harboured many a royal visitor. The pathetic Queen Margaret of Anjou sailed here in the hope of restoring her husband Henry VI to the throne; King Philip and Queen Joanna of Castile were swept in here during a storm and forced to stay over as they felt so ill; and, of course, Weymouth became George III's summer residence – a Regency statue in Coad stone by James Hamilton commemorates him on the front.

Mr Prowse and Mr Bennet started to promote the place as a resort in 1748 by building a few bathing huts north of the old harbour and Weymouth soon became the favourite holiday spot of a Cornishman, Ralph Allen, who owned quarries around Bath and became Weymouth's Lord Mayor. He spent up to three months a year here and asked friends to stay, including the Duke of York, brother of the future king. A touch of royalty was all the promoters needed. Weymouth took off, speculative builders moved in and, once it became frequented by the king at the end of the eighteenth century, the town mushroomed. There were balls and assembly rooms and gaiety everywhere. 'Many folk daily came into town,' according to a contemporary account in the 1790s, 'to see His majesty and the Court bathing in the sea-water half a furlong out from the shore. And some days the crowd could be so great on the sands that people are pushed into the water against their will.

The Budmouth Regis of Hardy's Wessex and the background to his novel *The Trumpet Major* is still glamorous and untawdry. It has an extraordinarily gentle atmosphere and feels content and settled.

Perhaps this is because of the lie of the hills around it. The Victorian novelist W. J. C. Lancaster, who wrote *The Secret of the Sands*, lived here but Weymouth's most famous son is James Thornhill, who painted the altar piece at St Mary's Church. He was born in what is now called the White Hart in Lower Bond Street, and was a close friend of Christopher Wren, who spent some time down here when he was in charge of the Portland Quarry, which produced the stone for St Paul's.

WINTERBORNE TOMSON

Dorset

SINCE some new Church of England clergymen want to turn their churches into centrally heated, Wilton-carpeted front rooms, with stacking chairs instead of pews, segregated changing rooms for the choristers, intensely bright sodium lighting, lavatories and movable exhibition screens, it is a relief to find a church whose dignity is allowed to remain intact.

Our churches belong to everyone. They are supremely beautiful and their fabric should be carefully safeguarded. A system set up in 1913 to do just this led to the formation of the Diocesan Advisory Boards – committees containing knowledgeable local aesthetes – but their powers seem to be diminishing as enthusiastic incumbents, driven by misdirected zeal and egged on by well-meaning villagers, take small aesthetic decisions into their own hands. Dulux is slapped on top of limewash with catastrophic effects as the walls can no longer breathe; local electricians are left to choose the light fittings or place wall-heaters at their convenience; churchyards are madly overtidied. Couldn't they take a leaf from Winterborne Tomson's book?

This is a church which makes you believe in God. It is worth driving miles to visit, for it cannot fail to lift your spirits with its simple perfection. Winterborne Tomson lies a stone's throw from the thundering Wimborne-to-Blandford road in meadowy country straddling the Winterborne – a chalk stream which dries up in summer. Some maps don't even mark it, noting only its biggest neighbours, Winterborne Zelstone to the east and, going upstream, Winterborne Anderson, Kingston, Whitchurch, Clenston, Stickland and Houghton. The church of St Andrew is set in a tiny hamlet next to a straggling farm of barns ancient and modern and a seventeenth-century farmhouse whose north façade is *far* more thrilling than its south. As you open the churchyard gate you see across the flat fields, beyond the poplars, the many gables and towering chimneys of Anderson Manor, a grand Elizabethan house of a strange plum-coloured brick with chalkstone dressings, tantalizingly unopen to the public.

From outside, the simple Norman church of lichen-covered brownstone rubble and flint resembles a small river tug-boat. Its walls have sloped outwards over the centuries. The inside is beyond expectation. It was renovated in the early eighteenth century and given box pews, a two-decker pulpit, and tester and chancel screen by William Wake, native of Blandford, later Archbishop of Canterbury. Everything is of oak which has bleached to the palest watery grey. There is a plastered wagon roof and three stone windows on the south side with clear-glass leaded lights. The church possesses an extraordinary calm, there is nothing that jars the eye – all is harmonious. There are no damp stacks of missionary leaflets, no guilt-inducing posters.

If this church is a monument to God then it is also one to the organizations that saved it. The first is the Society for the Protection of Ancient Buildings whose secretary, Mr Wake, restored the church in the early 1930s when it was in a very sad state of neglect. The money was raised from the sale of some of Thomas Hardy's manuscripts, which he left to the church because he was so fond of it. Mr Wake is buried in the churchyard. The second organization is the Churches Conservation Trust, which keeps 275 churches alive and well all over England that would otherwise become ruins. Each church is looked after by someone near by, and they are almost always open, or else the key is readily available. They feel very much alive, and they do not beome deconsecrated just because they are redundant. You can get married in one if you live locally. At least three services a year are held at most 'redundant' churches. At St Andrew's they occur at Whitsun, Harvest Festival and Advent, when the church is candlelit: there is no electricity.

WISTMAN'S WOOD

Dartmoor, Devon

WHEN it has rained for months and you want to go and live abroad, go to Dartmoor. Nowhere suits our wild winter weather better; nowhere is more relentlessly melancholy. The dark moorland will take you back thousands of years, with its ragged peaks appearing through the mist, its deep gloom and its stone circles, its ancient encampments and abandoned villages, but best of all it will reveal the weird and wonderful Wistman's Wood – a silent, unadulterated and secret place. If you go to the very middle of the moor, just up from Princetown and its prison, near Two Bridges, where the only two roads which cross the moor meet, there is a path which leads northwards towards Cocks Hill. From here it is a mile and half's walk along the side of a wide, long valley, gradually climbing into desolate country.

From a distance the wood looks like a patch of low scrub, grey-brown against the moorland, but as you approach it becomes gradually more magical. I think there is a fear of woods embedded in our subconscious from the days when the 'wildwood' covered the land. Today only nine per cent of the country is covered in trees and that is mostly in Scotland. Woods are tamer places now but they are still irrevocably laced into our literature and folklore. Wistman's Wood is not the sort of tall dark forest where Little Red Riding Hood and Hansel and Gretel get lost – it is where the knights of Arthurian legends struggle through tangled branches to perform heroic deeds and where Shakespearian heroes lose their way in 'this desert inaccessible, Under the shade of melancholy boughs'. Wistman's dwarf oaks bend in gnarled and twisted forms over outcrops of huge moss-covered stones. No modern grotto-maker could better this extraordinary landscape.

Woods get forgotten. They are places of mysterious beauty. Each wood has its own character and its own ancestry and, in the right circumstances, an awe-inspiring permanence – the Burren in Ireland has looked just the same as it does today for eight or nine thousand years, and parts of Wayland Wood in Norfolk, the supposed setting for 'Babes in the Wood' are truly primeval.

We are not woodland connoisseurs by nature – unlike the Scandinavians, who presumably have wood in their bones. Instead we are a nation obsessed by visiting houses and gardens, cathedrals and ancient monuments; seldom do we ever set out to visit a wood or ask about its age and history. In the spring we are more adventurous, seduced by primroses and bluebells, but Wistman's in the winter is as good as you can get. It is the 'dark but gentle ambush' described by Lousis MacNeice in his poem 'Woods':

> And always we walk out again. The patch
> Of sky at the end of the path grows . . .

and the valley opens out towards the long slow walk down to civilization and to the glories of the Two Bridges Hotel. When you reach the road it is waiting for you – a completely unspoilt eighteenth-century coaching inn beside the West Dart river. Inside there is a blazing fire in a huge stone fireplace. The roast beef they provide is famous. The walls groan with gleaming copper and brass and old photographs and upstairs there are Victorian brass beds. There is even a resident pianist. No wonder it was Vivien Leigh's favourite hotel.

YORK STATION

York

YORK has one of the most magnificent railways stations in Britain. Handsome, stalwart and true, it serves to remind us of what we have lost at Derby and Birmingham New Street. Look how timeless and adaptable it has been, how it has withstood bomb damage in the last war and how it remains a proud monument to those heroic Victorian railway engineers and architects.

Dr Beeching, one of this century's most misguided men, axed our branch lines and killed off hundreds of stations, leaving a trail of tragic devastation, but he did at least leave the main line system unwrecked. Helped by the valiant Victorian Society and English Heritage, listed stations are now safe from further degradation.

York Station was luckier than most. It survived without any radical change to its structure. It was northern pride that first put York on the railway map through the enlightened speculation of the legendary George Hudson. 'Mak' all t' railways cum t' York,' he said, and he was in a position to make it happen. Hudson was born at the village of Howsham near York, the son of a farmer. After leaving school he was apprenticed to a drapery shop in York when, unexpectedly, at the age of twenty-seven he inherited £30,000 from a distant relative. He was fascinated by railways and so he invested in North Midland Railway shares. From then on his career rocketed. First he became chairman of the Conservative Party in York, then town councillor, then alderman and, in 1837, Lord Mayor.

Meanwhile, Hudon's vision of the railway system was taking shape, and although his thinking was about seventy years ahead of his time, he managed to lay a sound basis for his life's ambition – to weld together a nationwide railway network. Stimulated by his civic success he struck out and supported new projects. Although there were vague rumblings along the tracks towards York in the 1820s and early 30s, it was not until the York and Midland Railway Company was formed, largely under Hudson's influence, that real progress was made. An Act of Parliament was obtained in 1836 and the first train ran from York's first station on 29 May 1839.

Hudson continued to engineer mergers and deals and seldom missed an opportunity to gain more track. When he heard about a new line being built from Newcastle and Berwick, he soon saw to it that York benefited: the York, Newcastle to Berwick line was born. (In 1853 it was amalgated with two other Hudson lines to become the North Eastern Railway.) By the mid 1840s, when the railway boom was at its height, Hudson had over a thousand miles of track under his command and interest in miles more. But as his operations extended, so he sailed closer and closer to the wind and he was eventually accused of fraud. The 'Railway King', as he was known, ended his days in poverty and disgrace.

Hudson had left an enormous legacy. York was its hub and its great showpiece. When the third and present station was built between 1873 and 1877 it was the largest in the world. The original design was by the official Northern Eastern architect, Thomas Prosser, who echoed John Dobson's earlier designs for Newcastle and also derived features from the roof at Paddington. Prosser retired in 1874 and was succeeded for two years by Benjamin Burleigh. But it was William Peachey who was ultimately in charge of the station's construction and is said to have modified and altered the design. The curving lines, which needed concentrically curving sheds, and the elegant sweep of roof above make the inside of York Station a magical and unforgettable place. When the station was finally opened in 1877, one of the North Eastern Railway shareholders deemed it 'a very splendid monument of extravagance'. It had cost £400,000 and is a truly beautiful building.

Four Short Tours

Around Alnwick

Around Cirencester

South-West Dorset

North Norfolk

AROUND ALNWICK

Ford

Bamburgh Castle

AROUND ALNWICK

Bamburgh

North Sea

Wooler

Chillingham

Embleton Bay

Rock

Cragside

Whittingham

Alnwick

Alnmouth

Edlingham

Alwinton

Harbottle

Warkworth

Cragside

0   5 miles

UNLIKE many southern counties, Northumberland still retains a fiercely individual character and its historical atmosphere is all-pervading. It must be the *quietest* of English counties with its massive tracts of hill and moor. The country roads here have as little traffic on them as in Ireland and great distances may be covered comfortably and without anxiety. The aura of feudalism is undeniable, for much of the landscape of Northumberland was created by the land-owning families, who planted woods and built many of its villages.

Warkworth

The great towering keep of this fifteenth-century castle standing high above the wide and wooded river Coquet is one of the wonders of Northumberland. The view towards it up the steep street of eighteenth-century houses, all of a piece, is breathtaking. Warkworth is one of the five great castles in the county, along with Northam, Bamburgh, Dunstanburgh and Alnwick. A ferry will take you upriver to the curious hermitage, where porch, cell, chapel, kitchen and dormitory are hewn from solid rock.

Alnmouth

This was once a thriving port, where smuggling was rife; John Wesley described it as being 'famous for all types of wickedness'. Now it is a quiet and unassuming little resort with a row of Victorian and Edwardian boarding houses tucked behind the village and facing away from the sea.

Embleton Bay

The sands at Embleton seem to go on for ever and you can see the silhouette of Dunstanburgh Castle to the south. In among the tumbling dunes are a scattering of little wooden beach huts, mostly built in the thirties by local families who came, and still come, for the day. They look utterly right. The National Trust, which owns the coastline, wants to pull them all down because it thinks they clutter up the view. Embleton golf course, among the dunes, is a 'wicked eighteen holes', according to locals. There is a good church and a village shop called Carrs and Watson, which will make up sandwiches to order, for your picnic.

Rock

It is easy to miss the best of this village, which lies down a narrow road to the left of the trees on the green. There is a row of picturesque mid-Victorian estate cottages with dormer windows, a school, a green, a lake and a seriously beautiful little church.

Bamburgh

Bamburgh Castle, set out on a promontory facing the relentless North Sea, lives up to one's expectations: it is 'perhaps the most tremendous spectacle of its kind in Britain', as Dr Thomas Sharp describes it in his *Shell Guide*.

Chillingham

The tiny church of St Peter, with its simple box pews, houses a breathtaking surprise – in the thirteenth-century Lady Chapel there is a little Georgian fireplace and the Grey table-tomb which must be the finest in the country. Beyond the church stands beautiful Chillingham Castle, set in an ancient park where the famous breed of wild cattle roam – directly descended from the white ox, they have never been domesticated.

Wooler

This small town is known by the locals as the 'centre of the universe'. Its hairdresser, Maison Crags, has recently changed its name to the Georgian Salon. There is a good second-hand book and furniture shop called Hamish Dunn.

Ford

Ford is one of the best and most surprising estate villages in England. It was built in the 1860s with exaggeratedly steep-gabled cottages – hardly the local style; in fact you could easily be in Kent. The village is the creation of the philanthropic and enormously rich Louisa, Countess of Waterford, on whose elaborate tombstone is written a quote from Dante: 'He who has seen this lady among others has seen perfection.' The *pièce de résistance* is the Lady Waterford Hall: the walls are plastered with her paintings of biblical scenes, which she began in 1862. She used all the inhabitants of the village as her models, so it is, in a sense, also a scene from nineteenth-century village life. See also pages 66–7.

Whittingham

A prosperous-looking village set around the infant river Aln, with limes and sycamores on its green and, nowadays, an air of peace as it is no longer on the main route from Newcastle to Edinburgh. There is an annual fair held here in September, the inspiration of the ballad 'Whittingham Fair'.

Harbottle and Alwinton

The last village in Coquetdale, with a rocky river, a ruined castle and hills all around. Beyond it lies Alwinton, the very last hamlet in Northumberland, with a lovely church from which a road winds up a narrowing valley and ends in the hills.

Cragside

A staggering and unbeatable house designed by Norman Shaw for Lord Armstrong. It was the first house in the world lit by hydro-electricity, which Lord Armstrong developed. There are forty miles of drives and footpaths in the grounds – it is worth travelling miles to explore them.

Edlingham

All that remains today of what was once a town is a romantic hamlet in a remote and picturesque valley on the edge of the moors. A church and castle have stood here for centuries. The present church is twelfth century, with a good Norman door, and the ruined castle is of of great beauty. There is a wonderful railway viaduct near by.

RECOMMENDED WALK

Seven miles west of Rothbury there is the tiny hamlet of Holystone in the Coquet valley, from where you can walk to Lady's Well, which has associations with St Ninian. Alternatively, the walk up the tiny lane from Chatton Moor between Bellshill and Chatton takes you up Kay Hill to Chillingham. You then skirt this, the most beautiful park in Northumberland, on a small road and thus reach Ross Castle, high above it, from whence there are huge views of the Cheviots, Lindisfarne and Bamburgh Castle.

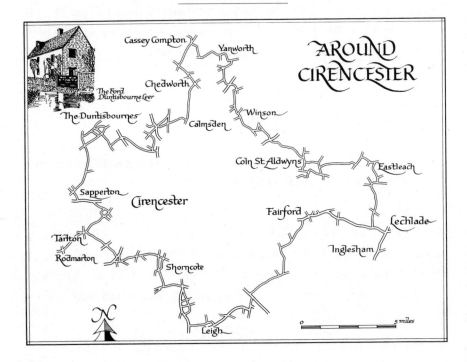

T HE cottages at Bilbury, the fine streets of Burford, Broadway and Stow, the gardens at Hidcote, Bourton-on-the-Water, the Slaughters and the Swells have been so stared at and marched around, so eulogized and sprinkled with antique shops, craft centres and tea shops, so calendared and postcarded that it is sometimes hard to find their magic. Undeniably beautiful all, the well-known wonders *should not necessarily be disregarded*; the following tour is an alternative. Apart from a slice of the Cotswolds, it takes in the lesser-known flat countryside around the upper Thames.

All Saints Old Chancel, Leigh

In this dead-flat watery countryside between Cricklade and Minety, where fritillaries proliferate secretly, lies the lonely chancel end of a church in the meadows. It is all that remains of the old church of Leigh (pronounced 'lie'). In the 1890s, against his own advice, the architect Mr Ponting was persuaded to remove the rest of the church to a drier and more convenient site in the village. The Leigh, as it is sometimes called, is hard to find up a track beside a farm and across two fields (map reference SU058928).

Fairford

The parish church contains some of the best medieval stained-glass in the country.

Lechlade

A lovely market town with an inexplicable amount of gazebos, a great 'wool' church (built on the proceeds of sheep farming) and punts and rowing boats for hire. Gliding up the narrowing Thames towards Inglesham is an unbeatable way to spend a couple of hours.

Inglesham

One of my top ten churches in the country – tiny, and deeply holy, it lies by the upper reaches of the Thames. William Morris performed a gentle restoration and the Churches Conservation Trust followed suit.

Eastleach

One of the prettiest villages in the Cotswolds, with its two medieval churches lying a stone's throw apart on either side of the river Leach.

Coln St Aldwyns

The villages of Quenington, Coln St Aldwyns and Hatherop, tumbling about little river valleys, are as pretty as could be.

Winson

One of the star villages in this picturesque valley, with its golden-stone manor house, Manor Farm and small early Norman church.

Yanworth

A pretty village with perfect front gardens and a good church in a secluded setting beside a farmyard.

Cassey Compton

There is an air of vanished splendour about this utterly beautiful, half-lost house in the Coln valley. To get the full magic it is essential to approach the valley down the tiny road through Chedworth, or from Yanworth through the loveliest of woods.

Chedworth Roman Villa

In the same Coln valley, on a well-chosen site are the remains of a Romano-British villa with two bath houses and a little museum.

Calmsden

Whiteway, a wonderful, straight Roman road radiating north-north-east from Cirencester, leads you high along a ridge above the wooded valleys of the Churn. Calmsden lies just off it, a tiny hamlet with a copious and perennial spring, over which is a beautiful fourteenth-century wayside cross on four steps. There is an old gabled manor, a later one built in the 1920s, and also this row of particularly pretty estate cottages with a glazing of diagonal and hexagonal panes.

Syde and Caudle Green

Wind up and down high-banked lanes to Caudle Green, which sits on a little plateau around a triangular village green, and look across the valley to Syde, another tiny village whose church, tithe barn, manor and cottages cling to the slope.

The Duntisbournes

A magical little river valley of perfect villages winds towards Cirencester; a wide ford in Middle Duntisbourne and a spectacular small church in Duntisbourne Rouse with scissor gates, perfect peace and an organ dedicated to Katherine Mansfield.

Sapperton

A fascinating village, where the Arts and Crafts movement thrived –
full of gabled cottages and fat topiary, with an eighteenth-century
church and the plainer end of the canal tunnel.

Tarlton

Here lies the Tunnel House Inn beside the entrance to the wondrous
canal tunnel, the greatest engineering feat in the world when it was
constructed in the late eighteenth century. See also pages 153–5.

Rodmarton

An Arts and Crafts manor house and an excellent chambered
neolithic long barrow at Windmill Tump.

Shorncote

In among the gravel pits and huge lakes, where Swindonians
windsurf and jet ski, and gravel lorries thunder and the hedges are
white with dust, lies a tiny pocket of peace and a small and near-
perfect twelfth-century church, sensitively restored by Butterfield in
1883.

RECOMMENDED WALK

A walk to take your breath away starts in Sapperton. Go straight to
the bottom of the valley and walk up northwards to Pinbury Park,
then west to Gloucester Beeches, down the road to Daneway and
back to Sapperton. Beautiful beyond compare.

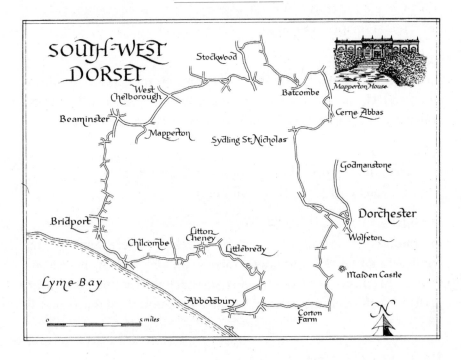

DORSET was once an important and heroic place, which the great hill forts on the chalk downs display, but since those days it seems to have been side-tracked and has little development save around Poole and Bournemouth. Dorset has remained a backwater, and this patch of country has that feeling. People only think of it as Hardy's Wessex, and they forget the great Dorset poet William Barnes who lived at Winterborne Came Rectory.

Wolfeton

A rambling Tudor house, reeking of romance, stranded in secret fields on the outskirts of Dorchester. Approach it off the A352 and go through the glorious medieval gatehouse, which looks decidedly French. Just beyond is the earliest riding house in England (1610).

Godmanstone

This village boasts the second smallest pub in England.

Sydling St Nicholas

The best way to approach this lovely village of thatched cottages is under the railway viaduct at Grimstone.

Cerne Abbas

The Romano-British version of Hercules stands erect, cut in the chalk above this satisfactory town among deep Dorset downs. Although it is teashopped to the hilt, it still retains its dignity.

Batcombe

Part of Batcombe's charm is that it is very difficult to find down deep, unmarked lanes. The church is glorious, set under the great folds of Batcombe Hill.

Stockwood (near Melbury Bubb)

Off the A37, south of Yeovil, just past the turning for Melbury Osmond, is perhaps the tiniest church in England, St Edwold's. It is 30 foot by 12 foot 8 inches and lies in a farmyard at the end of a track.

West Chelborough

Here, in the church you can see a moving monument of a young woman asleep with her daughter beside her. The village must be one of the remotest in Dorset and is well worth the little detour.

Mapperton

A golden Ham stone humdinger of an ancient house with spectacular gardens. See also pages 114–16.

Beaminster

Pronounced 'Be'mi'ster', as in the poet William Barnes's couplet:

> Sweet Be'mi'ster, that bist a-bound
> By green an' woody hills all round. . .

A Ham stone church dominates this picturesque town with a little green and many good houses. The country around is England's answer to Tuscany, but greener.

Bridport

One of the finest small towns in England. On the main street leading seawards if you walk through a small doorway painted pale grey, opposite the church, you come into a tiny courtyard where there is a Quaker meeting house and graveyard beyond.

Chilcombe

A hamlet set in high hills which tumble towards the sea. There is a tall, early manor farm and a little church.

Litton Cheney

A romantic rectory hides among the trees under a startlingly steep hill and there are some good cottages dotted about the village.

Littlebredy

Forever England – a cricket pitch beside the nineteenth-century Gothic manor house, a lake, the river Bride and a model village – all set in a particularly deep and dippy tract of Dorset.

Abbotsbury

This beautiful and bright golden-stoned village is dominated by the chapel of St Catherine, standing on a little tor like a mini Glastonbury. There is a vast tithe barn, a swannery and Chesil Beach beyond.

Corton Farm (between Portesham and Upwey)

These remains of a chapel belonged to a once large and noble house which, over the centuries, diminished to the farm it is today. The chapel stands in the farmyard, looking out across the mild Waddon vale before the sea. Don't miss Waddon Manor just up the road, more perfectly proportioned than almost any house I have ever seen. The main body of the house was burned down in the 1700s.

Maiden Castle

This, the finest Iron Age hill fort in the world, on the high chalk downs above Dorchester, remains miraculously undisturbed and awe-inspiring.

RECOMMENDED WALK

From Litton Cheyney walk to White Cross, turn left along the road and second right. Follow first a small metalled lane which turns into a bridle track up through the magical valley of Ashley Chase, then climb the hill and be knocked for six by the view of Abbotsbury and the sea below. The track down into the village feels ancient.

NORTH NORFOLK

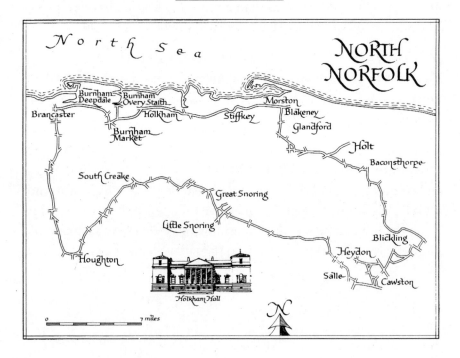

THE north Norfolk coast is strewn with wide marshes and tidal mud flats which only the locals know how to weave across. The waves are small, the beaches long, the skies as wide as wide can be. This patch of Norfolk has everything, from the greatest churches (there are 659 in the county) to the grandest houses. Almost the prettiest bit of country in Norfolk is around Houghton, which undulates gently and narrow, wide-verged roads (once drove roads), wend their way to handsome villages like Anmer. The use of brick and flint reaches artistic heights in almost every town and village.

Baconsthorpe
The romantic ruins of a large fifteenth-century fortified manor house partly surrounded by a lake, with gatehouse, bastions and curtain walls. Built by Sir Henry Heydon, recorder of Norwich.

Holt
A grand little market town which was completely burned to the ground in just three hours in 1706. Over the following two decades it was rebuilt to include many fine houses. It has good shops, including Simon Gough's second-hand books.

Glandford
A little estate village, built by the Jodrell family, of neat Dutch-gabled flint cottages. Just north of the splendid Edwardian church is the Shell Museum, containing a collection of shells brought from every part of the world, and other unexpected curios such as pottery, jewellery, ornaments, fossils and a magnificent embroidery.

Blakeney and Morston
Blakeney has a lovely High Street of brick-and-flint houses and was once a thriving port. It is famous for sailing now. Blakeney Point is a long stretch of sand dunes best approached from Morston, where a ravishing church sits on a slight prominence.

Stiffkey
The village street follows the course of the winding river and the marshes are full of sea lavender. The sandy track along the marshes towards Wells-next-the-Sea is irresistible.

Holkham
The great avenue planted with groups of ilex trees is for my money the finest in England. The house, designed by William Kent for the great farmer Coke of Norfolk, is of palace stature with an unbeatable enfilade of rooms.

Burnham Market

A pretty little flint town, where people in sailing clothes come to shop from holiday houses by the sea. All the Burnhams, and there are many of them, are pretty hot stuff. Burnham Thorpe is where Horatio Nelson was born. Burnham Overy Staithe harbour is beautiful.

Brancaster

A flint-and-brick village sprinkled with Edwardian holiday houses peters out into a sandy road leading across the marshes to the dunes and the famous golf course. Beyond are wide and endless sands.

Houghton

One of the two great Norfolk houses (Holkham being the other), it has been virtually untouched since it was built in the 1720s and is packed with Kent furniture. There are white deer in the park. See also pages 92–4.

South Creake

The glorious fifteenth-century church of St Mary cannot fail to amaze you. Clear glass throws light on the graceful piers and there is a spectacular hammer-beam roof above.

Little Snoring

Little Snoring church has a detached round tower, a wonderful Norman font and a vicar called Benjamin Lane, immortalized in stone as being 'the best Parish Priest as perhaps ever lived'; he died in 1744. Great Snoring church has good Commandment boards.

Salle and Cawston

Salle is a tiny village containing the largest and most magnificent church in the county. Seen across wide fields of corn it cannot fail to stop you in your tracks. Nearby Cawston church stands, by contrast, in a little country town and is also one of the best churches in Norfolk, with a hammer-beam roof complete with angels.

Heydon

A pretty, perfect brick village around a wide green with a dreamlike Elizabethan hall across the park. The village has been virtually untouched by the twentieth-century. See also page 86–8.

Blickling

Blicking Hall is a seventeenth-century red-brick house, mellow gabled and as perfect as can be. The long gallery has a Jacobean plaster ceiling. It has a wonderful garden and eighteenth-century orangery, and the park, designed by Humphry Repton, contains the Bonomi Mausoleum.

RECOMMENDED WALK

There could be none lovelier than the coastal path going east from Brancaster for as far as you care to travel. It is well marked and you can hire bicycles from the National Trust Information Centre at Brancaster Staithe harbour.

END NOTE

Do not embark on any of the tours without an Ordnance Survey map of the area because many of the suggested routes are on minor roads. The following reference books are also useful.

Churches in Retirement – A Gazetteer, J. L. Carr (HMSO)
Collins Guide to Parish Churches (Collins, 1992)
Collins Guide to the Ruined Abbeys of England, Wales and Scotland (Collins, 1993)
Gardens of England and Wales (The Yellow Book) (National Gardens Scheme)
Guide to English Heritage Properties (English Heritage)
Historic Houses, Castles and Gardens open to the Public (Reed Information Services)
The National Trust Handbook (National Trust)

The Acres, Norfolk

The castle and bailey gate at Castle Acre can be visited any time and are looked after by English Heritage, as is the priory, which is open all year 10 a.m–6 p.m.

Appledore, Kent

You could stay at Court Lodge, Appledore, a Victorian farmhouse overlooking the marsh: tel. (01223) 83403. Take along *Romney Marsh and the Royal Military Canal* by Richard Ingrams and Fay Godwin (published by Wildwood House Ltd, 1980).

Arbury Hall, Warwickshire

Arbury Hall is open from Easter to the end of September, Sundays only: gardens 2 p.m.–6 p.m; hall 2 p.m.–5.30 p.m.

The Ayots, Hertfordshire

Shaw's Corner, the home of George Bernard Shaw, belongs to the National Trust and is open from April to October, Wednesdays to Sundays and Bank Holidays.

Breamore, Hampshire

Breamore House and Countryside Museum (which contains superb recreations of various village workshops) are open from April to September on Tuesdays, Wednesdays, Thursdays, Saturdays, Sundays and all holidays from 2 p.m.–5.30 p.m.: tel. (01725) 22468.

Cartmel, Lancashire

Baines-Smith's bookshop is open seven days a week. Norman Kerr's high-class antiquarian bookshop is open by appointment: tel. (015395) 36247. The Uplands Hotel: tel. (015395) 36248. Holker

Hall is open from Easter to the end of October, every day except Saturday: tel. (015395) 58328.

Clevedon, Somerset

Clevedon Court belongs to the National Trust and is open from April to September on Wednesdays, Thursdays, Sundays and Bank Holiday Mondays 2.30 p.m.–5.30 p.m.: tel. (01275) 872257.

Clifton, Bristol

The Goldney Gardens are open twice a year under the National Gardens Scheme. See *The Yellow Book*.

Clovelly, Devon

Clovelly Court is open from Easter to October 9 a.m.–5 p.m., November to March 10 a.m.–4 p.m.: tel (01237) 431781.

Clun, Shropshire

Clun Castle is looked after by English Heritage and is open at any reasonable time. Admission is free.

Compton Beauchamp, Faringdon, Berkshire

The church is open daily. The house is *not* open to the public.

Dorney Court, Buckinghamshire

Dorney Court is open over the Easter Bank Holiday weekend, then until October on Saturdays and Sundays only from 2 p.m.–6 p.m. Home-made cream teas. Blooms of Bressingham have moved into the walled garden and brought a new lease of life. Here is a proper plant centre – no sundries, but 4,000 to 5,000 different varieties of plants and shrubs, beautifully arranged like an outside Harrods.

Edensor, Derbyshire

Stay in the Cavendish Hotel, Baslow: tel. (01246) 582311. Read *The Estate: A View From Chatsworth* (Macmillan 1990) by the Duchess of Devonshire, a moving account of a successful kingdom. Chatsworth is open from March to October daily, 11 a.m.–4.30 p.m.

Isle of Ely, Cambridgeshire
King's Cross Station enquiries: tel. (0171) 278 2477.

Ford and Flodden, Northumberland
Lady Waterford Hall is open from April to October, 10.30 a.m.–12.30 p.m. and 1.30 p.m.–5.30 p.m.: tel. (01890) 820224.

Fotheringhay, Northamptonshire
The Falcon pub at Fotheringhay is run by Mr and Mrs Alan Stuart and has extremely good fresh food at very low prices: tel. (0183 26) 254. The Castle Guest House is run by Stephanie Gould in the Victorian farmhouse next to the castle: tel. (0183 26) 200.

Frampton on Severn, Gloucestershire
Frampton Court and Manor Farm are open by appointment and the Gothic garden house is let on a holiday basis. Contact the estate office: tel. (01452) 740698.

Helmingham, Suffolk
The gardens and park are open to the public (the house is not) 2 May–12 September, Sundays only 2 p.m.–6 p.m., and there are cream teas in the old coach house. Further details from the estate office: tel. (01473) 890363.

Hemsley and Bransdale, Yorkshire
Rievaulx Terrace is owned by the National Trust and is open from April to the end of October: tel. (014396) 340. Bransdale is exemplarily managed by the Trust. Rievaulx Abbey ruins are in the care of English Heritage and are open from April to September 10 a.m.–6 p.m., October to March 10 a.m.–4 p.m. Of the many inns in Helmsley the Black Swan (or 'Mucky Duck', as locals call it) is the best for posh folk and the Crown for the less posh.

North-West Herefordshire

The park of Croft Castle belongs to the National Trust and is open to the public from April to the end of October. Brampton Bryan is emphatically *not*, although the garden of the house is open once a year and appears in *Gardens of England and Wales* (National Gardens Scheme). Daunt Books for Travellers is at 83 Marylebone High Street, London W1M 4A1: tel. (0171) 224 2295.

Heydon, Norfolk

The gardens of Heydon Hall, and the gardens of the Rectory, Grange and Old Cottage are open twice a year under the National Gardens Scheme. See *The Yellow Book*.

Hindon, Wiltshire

The Lamb: tel. (01747) 89573.

Houghton Hall, Norfolk

Open from Easter to the last Sunday in September on Thursdays, Sundays and Bank Holiday Mondays: gates open 12.30 p.m.–5 p.m.; house 1 p.m.–5.40 p.m.

Kelmscott Manor, Oxfordshire

Kelmscott Manor is open from 1 April to 30 September on Wednesdays 11 a.m.–1 p.m. and 2 p.m.–5 p.m. Access on Thursdays and Fridays may be arranged with the custodian: tel. (01367) 252486; or write to Kelmscott Manor, Kelmscott, Lechlade, Gloucestershire.

Kiftsgate Court, Gloucestershire

Kiftsgate Court is three miles east of Chipping Campden. There are plants for sale (be warned about where you plant your 'Kiftsgate' rose) and an exceptionally good tea room run by Doreen Dee in the old drawing room of the house. Open from April to September; Wednesdays, Thursdays, Sundays and Bank Holidays from 2 p.m.– 6 p.m.

The Lavant Valley, Sussex

Fox Hall, Britain's premier bedsitter, can be rented from the Landmark Trust, that unsurpassable organization started by John Smith. Ring or write to the Landmark Trust, Shottesbroke, Maidenhead, Berkshire: tel. (01628) 82592.

Mapperton, Dorset

The garden is open to the public from March to October daily 2 p.m.–6 p.m. House tours can be arranged for parties over fifteen in number and must be booked in advance: tel. (01308) 862645. The Bridge House Hotel, Beaminster, has particularly good food: tel. (01308) 862200.

Maud Heath's Casueway, Wiltshire

Kellaways Farm is open every year in June under the National Gardens Scheme, and by appointment from March to November: tel. (0124 974) 203.

The Peto Gardens, Iford, Wiltshire

The gardens (near Westwood, Bradford-on-Avon) are open in April and at Easter, on Sundays and from May to September daily, except Monday and Fridays 2 p.m.–5 p.m.

Prideaux Place, Cornwall

House open Easter Saturday for two weeks then Spring Bank Holiday to the end of September, Sunday to Thursday inclusive, 1.30 p.m.–5 p.m. There is an exceptionally friendly tea room offering clotted cream teas.

Restormel Castle, Cornwall

Restormel Castle is managed by English Heritage and is open from Good Friday to 1 April (whichever is earlier) to 30 September, 10 a.m.–6 p.m.

St Columb Major, Cornwall

Old Rectory: tel. (01637) 881318. Sylvia's Pantry in Fore Street is a good tea shop.

Sidmouth, Devon

Bovey House Hotel, seven miles east of Sidmouth, is a magical Elizabethan Devon manor house. You can get cream teas there or stay the night: tel. (01287) 680241.

Sir John Soane Museum, London

The Sir John Soane Museum is open every day except Monday 10 a.m–5 p.m.

Southend-on-Sea, Essex

Fenchurch Street Station enquiries: tel. (0171) 928 3100.

Teesdale, County Durham

The Morrit Arms, Greta Bridge: tel. (01883) 627232. Rokeby Park is open from June to August on Mondays and Tuesdays. The Bowes Museum: tel. (01833) 690606 (being refurbished at the time of writing).

Thrumpton Hall, Nottinghamshire

Thrumpton Hall is open by arrangement for parties and small conferences. For further information contact the Hon. Mrs Seymour: tel. (01602) 830333. The house and garden are open to the public once a year in September.

The Tunnel House Inn, Coates, Wiltshire

The Tunnel House Inn, Cirencester: tel. (01285) 770280. The Cotswold Canals Trust runs trips on Sunday afternoons and Bank Holidays until April (when the water levels permit): tel. (01285) 643440.

The Watts Gallery, Compton, Surrey

Compton is three miles from Guildford, south of the Hog's Back.

The financial future of the Watts Museum, which is a charity trust, is causing grave concern. Please go. It is open every day except Thursday 2 p.m.–6 p.m. (2 p.m.–4 p.m. from October to April), and on Wednesday and Saturday 11 a.m.–1 p.m.: tel. (01483) 810235. There is a tea shop.

Weymouth, Dorset
There is an excellent fish shop on the quay, where you can buy freshly boiled prawns. The ferry now only serves the Channel Islands.

Wistman's Wood, Dartmoor, Devon
Two Bridges Hotel, Dartmoor, Devon: tel. (01822) 890581.

York Station, York
The fastest trains from King's Cross to York take one hour and forty-three minutes (King's Cross enquiries: tel. (0171) 278 2477). The grand Italianate Station Hotel, which was built in 1853 by the York architect George Townsend Andrews, is now called The Royal York and has been taken over by the Principal Hotels Group: tel (01904) 653681. The Rail Riders' World, in the former North Eastern Tea Rooms, is one of the biggest model railway layouts in Britain, and the Railway Museum is close at hand.

Around Alnwick
Warkworth Castle is open from April to September, 10 a.m.–6 p.m., and October to March from Tuesday to Sunday 10 a.m.–4 p.m. Closed 24–26 December and 1 January: tel. (01665) 711423.
Lady Waterford Hall: see pages 66, 174 for details.
Cragside House is open from April to October, Tuesday to Sunday and Bank Holiday Mondays: tel. (01669) 20333/20266.
Bamburgh Castle is open from Easter until the last Sunday of October daily from 1 p.m.: tel. (016684) 208.

Around Cirencester

Chedworth Roman villa is open from March until the end of October, from Tuesday to Sunday and Bank Holiday Mondays, 10a.m.–5.30p.m., 3 November–5 December from Wednesday to Sunday, 11 a.m.–4 p.m.

South-West Dorset

Wolveton House is open from May to September, Tuesdays and Thursdays 2 p.m.–6 p.m: tel. (01305) 263500.

Mapperton House: see page 194 for details.

Abbotsbury: the swannery is open from May to September daily, 9.30 a.m.–4.30 p.m.

North Norfolk

The Shell Museum at Glandford is open Monday to Thursday 10 a.m.–12.30 p.m. and 2 p.m.–4.30 p.m., Fridays and Saturdays 2 p.m.–4.30 p.m.

Holkham Hall is open daily (except Fridays and Saturdays) from 30 May to 30 September 1.30 p.m.–5 p.m. Also Easter, May, spring and summer Bank Holidays, 11.30 a.m.–5.30 p.m.: tel. (01328) 710227.

Houghton: see page 192 for details.

Blickling Hall is open 27 March–31 October, Tuesday to Sunday and Bank Holiday Mondays: tel. (01263) 733084.

INDEX